PRIVATE EYE ANNUAL 2010

EDITED BY IAN HISLOP

HISTORY OF THE WORLD

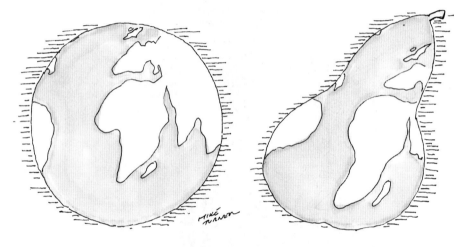

THEN   NOW

Published in Great Britain by
Private Eye Productions Ltd
6 Carlisle Street, London W1D 3BN
www.private-eye.co.uk

© 2010 Pressdram Ltd
ISBN 978-1-901784-53-4
Printed and bound in Great Britain
by the MPG Books Group
2 4 6 8 10 9 7 5 3 1

PRIVATE EYE ANNUAL 2010

EDITED BY IAN HISLOP

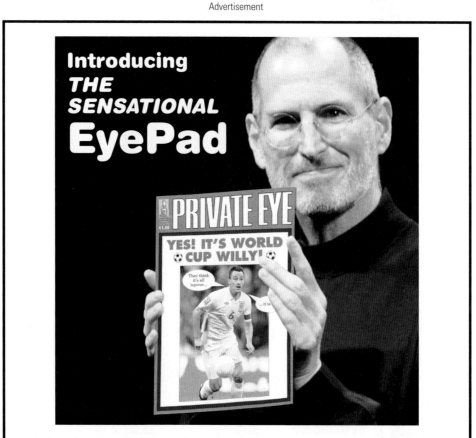

Introducing *THE SENSATIONAL* EyePad

The incredible technological breakthrough which will revolutionise the way you access information in the digital age.

It is:

◒ A4 size ◒ Lighter than a Laptop ◒ Touch sensitive

Simply scroll through the 'pages' of the EyePad with your finger and a world of content is at your command.

EyeApps include:

◒ Jokes ◒ Cartoons ◒ Stories ◒ Investigative Journalism
◒ Letter cancelling subscription ◒ Advert for Eye binders

And that's not all – look at these other amazing features:

◒ Unlimited battery time ◒ Scratch-resistant display
◒ Incredible 50-year memory
◒ Portable, foldable and can be rolled up to hit wasps

Yes! It's the EyePad at an amazing entry-level price of £1.50

Says Apple's Steve Jobless *"This spells the end of clumsy expensive old-fashioned e-reading devices. Frankly the EyePad renders **me** obsolete"*

CAMERON — 'I'M A ONE NOTION TORY'

by Our Political Staff **Des Railly**

THE Leader of the Conservative Party last night confirmed his allegiance to what he called "one notion Toryism".

He said, "This is a long and distinguished strand of Tory thinking and it consists of one notion."

He continued, "The notion is that I want to win and I will say anything to ensure that this happens.

"One notion Toryism means that the whole nation unites in believing that I am a possible Prime Minister and no one is left out thinking that I am an obvious PR man and chancer."

Traditional Conservatives were quick to wake up and ask whether Mrs Thatcher was still on the throne before criticising their young leader. Said one:

The Camerons Are Coming

"Cameron is abandoning mainstream Tory traditions such as losing. We have had a venerable succession of Tory leaders who believed in the power of losing including such great figures as William Hague, Michael Howard and Iain Duncan Cough. It would be a tragedy to throw all that away simply by trying to win the election."

Mr Cameron Rejoices in the Knowledge that the Sun is Shining on him

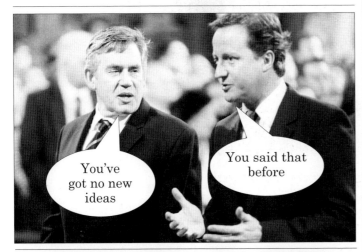

You've got no new ideas

You said that before

BRITON GETS JOB SHOCK

by Our Industrial Staff **Phil Post**

A BRITISH worker stunned officials yesterday when he was employed by a local firm to do something in return for a wage.

Said a spokesman for the government, "This is outrageous. We have created over one million jobs for foreign workers and now this firm has irresponsibly hired a man who is quite obviously British."

He continued, "Had the firm in question bothered to investigate the labour market, they would have found a large number of suitably qualified Poles, Ukrainians, Somalis, Nigerians, Kyrgyzs, South Africans, Apache Indians or, indeed, Inuits who could easily have done the job.

Dole Not Role

"This is a slap in the face for Gordon Brown's policy of guaranteeing unemployment for all British workers."

PRESCOTT WILL BE LABOUR'S AL GORE – What You Will Hear

66 NOW that I have had the honour of being appointed as European Super-Czar In Charge Of Climactic Change and made a Chinese Professor of Climatography, I am determined to stop carbon footsteps and clamp down on omissions to save the planet from a hologram brought about by globalised warning and people leaving their TVs on standstill all night and that is why I have flown out here to China, or wherever I am, to lay down a few basic elemental targets to get everyone sorted out on this crucialised issue before all the polar bears melt away before our eyes, and the sea levels rise thousands of feet, engulferating whole polupations such as Bangalore and Amsterjam... er... we can all *(cont. p. 94)*

THE SCOTTISH SCUNNERS MAKING SPECTACLES OF THEMSELVES!   Fountain and Jamieson

IS IT TRUE, MR OPTICIAN, IS PA BROON'S EYESIGHT REALLY DETERIORATING?

OPTICIAN

AYE, AH'M AFRAID IT'S TRUE, YE KEN...

JINGS!

...NO MATTER HOW HARD HE TRIES...

HE CANNAE READ THE WRITIN' ON THE WALL!

ROSE TINTED SPECTACLES

PA BROON 4 EVER

YOU ARE DOOMED

Z...Q...X ...T?

HENRY DAVIES

FLEET STREET LEGEND DEAD

Nation Mourns

by Lunchtime O'Booze

MAKE no mistake – Keith Waterhouse was a legend in his lifetime and was recognised as one of the most prolific drinkers of his generation.

It is estimated that during his long career, Keith drank over 25,000 bottles of champagne, plus countless bottles of white wine, red wine, beer, cider and Scotch.

He was such a dedicated boozer that by eleven o'clock in the morning he had already dashed off a Jeroboam of Taittinger and several dozen doubles of McHackey's Fine Old Highland Malt ("a wee dram afore ye have another dram").

He once famously said, while sitting in a corner of one of his favourite pubs, *The Old Hack in a Bush*, in Watkins' Court, just off Fleet Street, "No day is complete unless I have several dozen empty bottles to show for it".

But those who knew Keith well were aware that he had another life, writing countless plays, novels and newspaper columns *(cont. p. 94)*

On other pages

'BONKING TAX WILL HURT CAPITAL,'
Says Johnson

LONDON Mayor Boris Johnson yesterday condemned the government's proposal for a 'Bonking Tax'.

Speaking on the BBC's Andrew Gurn show, the Tory Mayor blustered, "It would only work with an international bonking agreement. A supertax on bonking would only encourage Britain's top bonkers, like myself, to go overseas and bonk elsewhere.

"We should be removing all obstacles to bonking, so that international bonkers should be encouraged to bally well bonk over here."

Mr Johnson later added, "A banking tax? Oh well, that's a tommy rot idea too."

Status of Kerry Katona officially raised to 'troubled'

by **Michael Heat**

THE OFFICIAL status of Kerry Katona has now been raised from "tearful" to "troubled", *Heat* magazine has said, following crisis talks with her ex-husband.

The level was last raised in April, which meant losing a lucrative advertising deal was "highly likely". The latest upgrading means there is a "strong possibility" of the star going into complete meltdown, which could even lead to the public becoming increasingly bored.

Celebrity experts have said Katona's level was "under constant review" and could go down again if it was felt appropriate. .

INFORMATION: How does the status level system escalate?
● Worried
● Tearful
● Troubled
● Critical
● Winehouse

"We've got to tighten everybody else's belt"

That New Oxford Dictionary of Quotations

Those New Additions In Full

NOW, alongside such geniuses as Albert Einstein, Winston Churchill and Oscar Wilde, the modern generation will at last have their say in the all-time pantheon of fame that is the Oxford Dictionary of Quotations.

What You Will Read

Jamie Oliver *"Lovely jubbly"*

Paris Hilton *"I'm Paris Hilton"*

Sir Stephen Fry *"Bless"*

Wayne Rooney *"I was never offside, ref"*

Sir Alan Sugar *"You're fired"*

Rabbi Lionel Blue *"Hullo Brian, hullo Sue"*

Prince Harry *"Yah"*

Hilary Clinton *"Vote for me"*

Gordon Ramsay *"Fuck off"*

Yes, these are just some of the immortal quotations of our time that sum up the spirit of the age we live in and will be treasured as a source of wisdom before being taken to the local Oxfam shop where they will remain on the shelf for generations to come.

"Fantastic. Party of four"

PARENTS TO BE VETTED 'BEFORE TAKING CHILDREN TO SCHOOL'

by Nanette State

A NEW independent body appointed by the Home Office, the Supervisory Parental Standards Agency, headed by a senior civil servant will enforce strict new controls on parents who want to take their children to school.

Shock

Said Sir Peter Dimme, chair of the new agency, "Our primary aim is to protect vulnerable children. Our primary aim is to protect vulnerable children. Just keep saying this whatever they ask. Oh, sorry, I shouldn't have read that bit out."

He continued, "Any adult volunteering to escort his or her children to their place of education should clearly undergo intensive waterboarding at a secret Guantanamo-style vetting centre in order to force them to confess that they are paedophiles."

Sir Peter was then taken away by two men in white coats.

Electric shock

In response to criticism of the new regulations, the government has announced another new agency to vet the suitability of those appointed to chair vetting agencies.

Said new chair Lady Daphne Hare-Brain, "You're obviously a paedo, aren't you? I can tell at once you know."

On other pages

Those agencies in full… p2-94.

⚽ ENGLAND WIN WORLD CUP

by Our Football Correspondent Lunchtime O'verexcited

YES! We've done it! Football has come home at last as our glory boys showed the rest of the world who is number one!

Make no mistake, Lamps, Stevie Gee and the Spud-faced nipper will go down in legend as not only the greatest footballers who have ever played, but the men who ended forty years of hurt to give England the ultimate prize of the World Cup.

Crow-atia

All that remains is for the boys to play a few matches and beat some other teams, but there is no getting away from the fact that yesterday at Wembley history was made and WE WON THE WORLD CUP.

They think it's all over – it is now.

Late Score

Unhatched chickens **5**

Hatched chickens **1**

Those LIDLs In Full

LIDL, downmarket supermarket peddling cheap goods.

ROD LIDL, downmarket columnist peddling cheap articles in the Sunday Times.

RICHARD LIDL JOHN, downmarket columnist peddling cheap articles in the Daily Mail.

LIDL BRITAIN, downmarket TV show peddling cheap jokes on the BBC.

MIDL BRITAIN, downmarket country which *(That's enough, Ed.)*

7

Neasden named as 'cradle of human race'

by Our Science Staff **Ann Thropologist** and **Miss I.N.G Link**

FOR centuries it has been believed that Africa was the birthplace of the human race, but sensational recent finds on a north-west London building site have led archaelogists to hypothesise that in fact the first human beings in the history of the world lived over 100 million years ago in the suburb of Neasden.

It was three weeks ago that workmen digging the foundations of the new Tesco Express on the North Circular-Dollis Hill interchange unearthed a skull which archeologists identified as belonging to a hitherto unknown "missing link" in the line of hominid descent.

"Sid, as we call him," said Professor Lee Kee of Shanghai, "is by far the most primitive form of human life ever discovered. The skull suggests that *homo neasdenicus* had a very small brain, and was only capable of semi-articulate grunts such as, 'come on, you squirrels' and 'the ref's a bastard'."

Where You Can See the Neasden Skull

Neasden Public Library, open Tuesdays 11-12, except Tuesdays.

Reprinted by permission of the Neasden and Dollis Hill Independent.

A slobbering sexist xenophobe who wouldn't get a column today

by Dr Johnson (no relation)

Sir, it must be apparent to any man who contemplates the figure of Mr. Boris Johnson that such a man would never be granted employment on a respectable 18th century organ of opinion such as the Gentleman's Magazine.

For consider not only his unseemly and adulterous dalliance with divers ladies of the town but also reflect upon his opinions of picaninnies, the good citizens of Liverpool and the gentlefolk of Portsmouth which are scarcely those of a classically educated gentleman but more resemble those of an illiterate hansom cab driver who would have all persons who have offended him for whatever reason taken to Tyburn and strung up like murderers or common felons on the public gallows before a baying mob claiming it is the only language (continued 1794.)

Let's Parlez Franglais!

Numero 94

EU Foreign Ambassador Baroness Ashton brushes up her language skills after criticism from the French

Baroness Ashton: Teachez-moi les essential phrases pour mon top euro-job, s'il vous plait.

Le Teacher: Ok! Repetez after me... "Yes, Monsieur. No, Monsieur. Trois bags pleins, Monsieur".

Baroness Ashton: Oui, sir. Non, sir. Three sacs full, sir.

Le Teacher: Parfait! Vous êtes un genius! Et maintenant, "Vive La France!".

Baroness Ashton: Deutschland über alles.

Le Teacher: Non, non, non *(cont. p. 94)*

GLENDA SLAGG

Fleet Street's Original WAG!!!

■ PUHLEASE no Mr BBC man, not Chris Evans for Breakfast?!?? This four-eyed, ginger-haired egomaniac will never fill Tel's king-size slippers!?!! What's Cheesy Chris ever done to deserve Radio 2's top hot seat!??!! He's an irritating, juvenile and from now my snap, crackle and pop will be going soggy!!?! Ughh!! Call me a TOG if you like – that's Turn Off Ginger!?! Geddit!??!

■ CALL me a TOG!!! That's Turn On Ginger, geddit!!?! Thank Gawd the Beeb have given us Classy Chris and we've seen the last of Tedious Tel!!?! From now on it's snap, crackle and pop all the way with the wisecracking wonderkid instead of Mr Blarney, the winking wag in a wig!!?!

■ HERE THEY ARE – Glenda's Harvest Festival Hunks!?!

● **Heston Blumenthal.** OK, you make everyone sick, but not me!?!! I'll have you for starters and main course too!!?! Fancy a Fat Duck, big boy??!!

● **Sir Elton John.** OK, so he wants a Ukrainian boy!!?! Who doesn't!?!! But if it doesn't work out, I'm always free!!?!

Byeee!!

"For God's sake – you only live for 24 hours, and you've spent 23 of those writing a blog about it!"

K.J.Lamb

That Poisoned Fat Duck Menu In Full

Pee Soup
Dressed Crap

– ✳ –

Grilled WC Bass
Baked Turdbot
Down-the-pan Fried Oysters with Shit-ake Mushrooms

– ✳ –

Sewage Pudding
or
Toilet Roll

– ✳ –

To drink:
Poo-willy Fumé 2009
(We get the idea. Ed.)

Now wash your hands, please

SPORTSMAN DOESN'T CHEAT SHOCK

by Our Unsporting Staff

THE world of rugby, football, motor racing and all the others were rocked to their foundations with the sensational revelation that a sportsman had not dived, pretended to be cut nor deliberately crashed his car.

Said a spokesman for sport, "The sportsman is not representative of the vast majority of cheats who do their very best to compete in a dishonest way".

Late News

● Sportsman doesn't abuse official or assault opponent either.

GNOMEBY'S
LONDON

A collection of Royal memorabilia, formerly the property of Prince and Princess Michael of Kent

———— Lots include ————

One ornamental red silk chair, as sat in by the late Duke of Kent at the Coronation of George VI

One red leather-style chair, as sat in by Princess Michael of Kent during the Coronation Street omnibus edition

One de-luxe gentleman's razor from Mitchell & Webb of Bond Street (as never used by HRH Prince Michael)

One complete set of seven thousand unsold copies of "The History of Royal Trouserpresses" by Princess Michael (Fawn & Cringe £29.99)

One eviction notice signed by Her Majesty the Queen, bearing the message "Get out of Kensington Palace by Friday, Pushy, or I'll send the bailiffs in"

One pair jack boots, part of the full dress uniform of an Obergruppenführer in the Waffen SS. As worn by Baron von Ribena-Schnitzel in the invasion of Alsace-Lorraine-Heggezy

One car boot belonging to the estate of Prince Michael

GNOMEBY'S
*What a **lot** of rubbish!*

Wedding of the Century

Ken & Em
How They Are Related

Ken Livingstone	Emma Beal
Erik The Red	Lady Emma Hamilton
Ethelred The Ken	Lady Emma Soames
Salamander The Magnificent	Sir Robert Beal
Sir Isaac Newt	John Peel
Dr Livingstone	D'Ye-Red-Ken-John-Peel?
Princess Michael Of Ken	Princess Bea-l
Red Adair	Ian Beale (off *EastEnders*)
Fred Astaire	Eminem
High Street Ken	M&S
Kenneth Branagh	**Emma Thompson**

That Humanist Service In The Reptile House In Full

Zookeeper: Do you, Ken, take this Emma to be your partner in a very real sense in the sight of all these newts.

Ken: The whole point about Boris is that he never says "yes" to anything, he's even had to cancel his scrapping of the congestion charge which I warned would happen, when I was Mayor and...

Zookeeper: May I just interrupt you there and ask you again if you take this woman to be...

Ken *(interrupting)*: I'm glad you asked that question, Londoners made a serious mistake in voting for Boris Johnson and whilst we are on the subject of promises, Boris' promise to bring back the Routemaster failed to materialise like all his other promises.

Newts: Zzzzzzzzz
(Service continues for several hours)

Easy Recipes from the Eye

No. 94. An Apple

Ingredients
One apple
Directions
1. Buy an apple
2. Eat it
Serves one

Tomorrow: A can of coke.
Have you got a favourite recipe? Send it in to Eyeeasy.co.uk

Those Afghan Election Results In Full

Kabul South: P.J.Q. Karzai *(no relation)*, Ruling Party: 49 votes. A.R.J. Antibakhanda, End Corruption Now Party: 251,600 votes.

Ruling Party hold seat. President's brother elected.

Helmand East: M.L.V. Karsai *(no relation)*, Ruling Party: 0 votes. Other candidates *(all deceased)*: 0 votes.

Ruling Party gain from Taliban. President's brother-in-law's friend's best man elected unopposed.

Full results next year.

"He's constantly on the look out for signs that the caliphate has been established"

MAZURKE

BRITAIN CLOSING DOWN SALE!

All items previously the property of the taxpayer now on offer due to bankruptcy

1000's of lots at knock down prices including:

☆ **CHANNEL TUNNEL** – yours for £10!

☆ **STUDENT LOANS** – take them away, please. We'll let you have them all for 99p!

☆ **NELSON'S COLUMN** – make us an offer!

☆ **BEEFEATERS** (set of ten) 2p each!

☆ **NORTH CIRCULAR** – no offer refused!

YES, EVERYTHING MUST GO – EXCEPT GORDON BROWN

9

HOW KNACKER SAVED WORLD FROM DISASTER 'WORSE THAN 9/11'

by Our Writing-down-what-the-police-tell-us Staff **Phil Notebook**

FOLLOWING the sensational conviction of three top terrorists, found guilty of plotting to create a 9/11-style outrage by blowing up 79 airliners simultaneously, Inspector 'Knacker of the Yard' Knacker yesterday paid tribute to himself and his staff for their foiling of the so-called 'Lucozade Bombers'.

Said Knacker, "It was a classic case of good old-fashioned police work – solid forensic analysis of all available leads which resulted in the apprehension of these world-class criminals."

When pressed for further details, Knacker explained, "The big breakthrough came when we got a phone call from our colleagues in Pakistan."

"It was an Inspector Nakerstani from Islamabad who gave us the vital tip-off that we needed."

The inspector then read out a transcript of the conversation which was to prove the turning point of the entire investigation.

"Nakerstani: We have reason to believe that three very dodgy fellows from your country are planning to do terrible things to aeroplanes with hydrogen peroxide. If you have pencil and paper I can give you their names and addresses. They are coming home on a plane to England and good riddance to them, we are all saying".

High Wycombe Explosive

Knacker went on to explain how, thanks to tried and tested procedure, he had managed to copy out the names and addresses correctly, and he and his men had then gone to their addresses and arrested them.

"A search of the premises in question," he continued, "led to the discovery of a pile of bomb-making equipment (e.g. Coca Cola, shampoo etc.) plus a set of videos in which the terrorists explained how they were going to blow up the aeroplanes and thus commit suicide."

■ Full story and pics: pp 1-94

WAR ON TERROR LATEST

US To Invade High Wycombe

■ Full story and pix, 94

St Vincent of Cable

AND THERE lived in those times a good and holy man named Vincent, who was much loved by the people for his wisdom and gifts of prophecy. Like Noah of old, Vincent alone in the kingdom

warned the people of the great storm that was about to come upon them, when all the banks would fail and everyone in the land would be drowned in a sea of debt.

And it came to pass, even as Vincent had foretold. And his reputation waxed so great that he became known as "Saint Vincent", and his followers begged him to take one of the most powerful positions in the country (leadership of the Liberal Democrat Party).

But so unworldly was Vincent that he turned them down, saying, "I am old and full of years, and I would not look good on television, unless of course you can get me on Strictly Come Dancing."

CLASSIC FAIRY STORIES
THE FRANGLAIS EDITION

The Princess And The Frog

by Former President **Giscard d'Estaing**

UNE FOIS upon a time, une très handsome grenouille (i.e. moi) was sitting à un grand banquet next to une belle Princess qui s'appellait Le Princess Diana de Cardiff (Gettez-vous it?).

Et guessez what!

La Princess a tombé tête over heels en love avec la grenouille immediatement.

"Vous êtes la plus sexy old grenouille I've ever recontré," elle purred.

Et puis elle à kissed le vieux frog.

Et zap! Paff! Zut alors! "Je didn't expect that!" exclamé la belle Princesse de Wales.

Because connaissez-vous what had happened, mes enfants?

Oui! C'est vrai! La vieux grenouille ne turned pas into un handsome President.

Non! He turned into un very piss-pauvre noveliste instead!! Quelle surprise!

Et tout le monde laughed happily ever après. (Surely 'lived'? Ed).

© The Late Kilometres Kington.

POLICE LOG

Neasden Central Police Station

0815 hrs The Station Armed Response Unit answered an urgent distress call from a guest at the St Christopher bed and breakfast establishment in Somerfield Road. The lady in question, Mrs Doreen Burqa, a devout Moslem, claimed that she had been racially and religiously abused by the guest house proprietor, Mr Timothy Wetherspoon, who had offered a "full English", including a rasher of bacon and a pork sausage, in breach of the Public Order (Racial and Religious Harassment) Regulations 2007.

On arrival, the team led by Det Sgt Farringdon arrested Mr Wetherspoon, who was unfortunately injured while being assisted into the back of a police car. He was charged with 17 offences (see above), which he did not deny owing to the fact that he was unconscious.

The accused unfortunately died before admitting his guilt, and his wife's request that her husband should be given a Christian burial was refused on the grounds that it would be a provocative and inflammatory act which would give further offence to Mrs Burqa and the entire Moslem community.

Mrs Burqa was awarded £315,000 ex-gratia compensation for the insult which had been offered to her religion, and the widow Mrs Wetherspoon was ordered to sell the guest house to raise the money required.

A Mrs Wetherspoon, of no fixed abode, was later found wandering along Morrison Road and arrested for vagrancy.

1232 hrs WPC Turnham-Green, acting as desk officer, turned on the station answerphone to check on any messages received since the beginning of the month. There were only 158 of these, all of which were from a female member of the public who was claiming that she and her family were being "terrorised" by a gang of youths wielding knives and throwing bricks through her window. Fortunately her final message indicated the intention of the complainant to kill herself and her family, thus obviating any need for further investigation. The case is therefore now closed.

1428 hrs All officers were summoned to sign a suitable card of congratulation, purchased from Mr Patel's Carderama in Lidl Road, to be sent to our colleagues in the Chelsea Firearms Division, following the official decision that no further action should be taken against them concerning their successful resolution of the Markham Street siege. The card showed a sportsman shooting a grouse, to which PC Hainault had added the witty handwritten comment "Gotcha!"

Due to the current industrial dispute affecting the postal industry, it was decided that the card should be delivered by hand. PC Perivale was therefore instructed to carry out a person-to-person delivery using squad car N94. In the course of executing this duty, PC Perivale again broke the station record (148 mph) whilst travelling down Willesden High Street, despite being impeded by a number of pedestrians, several of whom sadly underwent a terminal accident experience.

DIGNITAS WELCOMES RULING

THE Dignitas Clinic in Switzerland say they expect business will be booming following the Government's recent clarification of the law on assisted suicide.

Said a spokesman, "That's why, for a limited time we're offering two lethal injections for the price of one. Yes that's two great lethal injections so you can help two family members not to be a burden any longer. What an offer! Bump one off. Get one free." *(Reuters)*

Your assisted suicide tick-box guidelines in full

I am terminally ill and want to die by:

☐ **a)** Lethal injection

☐ **b)** Knife-wielding hoodie

☐ **c)** Strictly Come Dancing being extended to run over two hours

☐ **d)** Listening to Gordon Brown's Conference speech

☐ **e)** All of the above

EYE TV

What Celebrity Raped Katie Next

Living TV Tues. 9.00pm

In her new distorted reality show, former glamour model Katie Price makes yet more vague sensationalist accusations of rape against unnamed celebrities to sell a few tabloid newspapers *(Surely 'raise the level of awareness about violence against women'? Ed.)*

Eye Rating: You'll feel like you've been violated.

"It's shrunk again"

The Secrets of the Mary Rose

What they found on the 500 year old Tudor warship

● **Wooden tankard**

● **Nit comb**

● **Sailors' clogs**

● **2 tickets to Mousetrap**

● **Best of Andy Williams song sheet** (including Moon River)

● **Bruce Forsyth's joke book**

● **Ming Campbell election leaflet** (Vote For Ye Liberal Democrats)

● **Invitation to join *Oldie* cruise on the Mary Rose with guest speakers Richard Ingrams, Mavis Nicholson and Beryl Bainbridge** *(That's enough, Ed)*

HOW TIMES CHANGE

REFERENDUM PARTY 1997 | CONSERVATIVE PARTY 2009

Vote for me because I'm incredibly rich

Nursery Times

TOAD BIOGRAPHY SHOCK

by **Kenneth Grahame-Green**

LOVABLE rogue or despicable Fascist? That's the question raised by the publication of a new biography of Mr Alan Toad of Toad Hall.

With his love of fast cars, fast women and leaders of the Nazi Party, Toad was a larger-

than-life character who divided opinion wherever he went.

Scoop! Scoop!

One weasel told *Nursery Times*, "The book is quite right. Toad was a Fascist, an aristocratic snob, who despised weasels and wanted us to be wiped out."

Yet a close friend, Sir Adrian Moley, defended him, saying, "I don't recognise this picture of Toad. He was generous, warm-hearted and kind. On his deathbed he converted to Catholicism and is now a saint."

ON OTHER PAGES ● Cow says "I saw water on Moon" **2** ● Waitrose to buy Royal Organic Tart business **3** ● Gingerbread House price to rise **4**

GLENDA SLAGG

The Brighton Belle!?!! (Geddit?!!?)

■ **HANDS OFF** dishy film-maker Roman Polanski!??!! He's the sexy septuagenerian sex offender, stoopid!?!! OK, so he raped a 13-year-old!!?! But it was all a long time ago – and who cares??!? And just think of all those fab films he's given us in the meantime *[Note to sub: fill in names of fabulous films]*. Have those Swiss cops gone cuckoo or what?!!? Why arrest the poor old soul now?? Roman's suffered enough and served his debt to society by living in exile and making such films as *[Note to sub: fill in names of more fabulous films]*.

■ HATS OFF to the Swiss police!!?! At last they've caught Polanski the Paedo as he lurked and smirked in his alpine eyrie!!?! For too long the Dirty Director has evaded justice, living a life of luxury in the land of cuckoo clocks and Toblerone!?!! Now at last he will be forced to pay his debt to society and rot in a Swiss jail, kept awake by cuckoo clocks and living only on Toblerone!!?! *(You've done this bit. Ed.)* And being a Kiddie Kriminal is not Polanski's only krime!?! (Geddit?) What about all his rotten old films?!? Like *[Note to sub: fill in name]* or *[Fill in another name]* or *[Fill in again]*!!?!!

■ **STRICTLY Come Off it Mr Auntie Beeb!?!!** What's Alesha Dixon doing a-judgin' and a-fudgin' on

the panel instead of our Arlene!?!! Gor blimey – she's hopeless!?! She doesn't know her cha-chas from her elbow!?? Geddit?! Here's Glenda's marks, darling! Zero! Nil! Nought! and Zilch!!? Geddit?!? Now Foxtrot off, sweetheart!?!

■ LEAVE her alone, Mr Pressman!?!! Allurin' Alesha, I'm talkin' about!?!! Just 'cause she's young 'n' sexy, it seems the whole country's got it in for her!!?! OK, so she isn't a professional hoofer!!?! Hoo-fer-gawd's-sake cares!!?! (Geddit?!?) Honestly – you'd think she'd started World War Three and caused the credit crunch!!? Well, here's Glenda's score!?!! Ten! Ten! Ten! Eleven!!? So just fandango off Mr Media and Alesha alone!?!! (Geddit?!?) We love her – waltz and all!??!? *(You're fired. Ed.)*

■ HERE THEY ARE – Glenda's Fit Fall Fellas!?!

● **Lembit Opik.** OK, so your uncle was a Nazi!?! You're still my Mr Extreme Right!??!

● **Richard Mawhinney.** OK, you're married to Baroness Scotland – when she's in jail I'll come and *do* for you!?!! Geddit?!!

● **Ben-Hur.** OK, so you're 2000 years old but I bet you can still give a girl a good ride?!? Even if it is only two minutes?!!! (Geddit?)

Byeee!!

"I much prefer the quieter route across the Alps"

'I SHOULDN'T HAVE GIVEN HER A JOB,' Admits Brown

by Our Political Staff **Selina Scotland**

THE PRIME MINISTER, Gordon Brown, today came clean and admitted he had hired a woman of Commonwealth origin to act as his Attorney General without "making any checks whatsoever" on her bona fides.

"I was wrong," he said, "but it was an easy mistake to make. I am a busy man and she looked exactly the sort of woman who would clean things up for me and make sure everything was tidy from a legal point of view."

Look Back In Tonga

The woman was named as Patricia Scotland, who claimed to have all the qualifications necessary to be Attorney General.

"The Baroness", as she liked to be called, had very good references from a Mr Blunkett for whom she had done "excellent work".

However, Mr Brown now confessed that he had made "a technical error" in employing someone who made him look like an idiot.

But he said that employing the Baroness "was no worse than not paying the Congestion Charge or invading Iraq" *(cont. p. 94)*

A Doctor Writes

GUTENTAG. As ein doctor, how you say, some people are asking me all ze time, "Can you speak English, please?"

Ze answer is not so good, I'm telling you. I haf only just come in from Frankfurt zis morning. And I am very tired. So my question to you is: "Vere ze hell am I? Und vat exactly is zis diamorphine zat you are vanting?"

© A Doctor

If you are worried that your doctor does not speak English, you should move to Germany at once.

12

THIS WEEK

BEN BRADSHAW
Secretary of State for Culture, Media and Sport

Do you have many spoons?

Not as many as people at the BBC. They've got hundreds of spoons, thousands probably, it's a disgrace.

Do you have a favourite spoon?

No, I'm not biased, unlike the BBC who are so pro Tory, it's a disgrace.

So, you're saying you don't have a favourite spoon?

Now you're putting words into my mouth – just like the BBC who are, frankly, a disgrace.

OK, let's put it another way. Do you...?

Just like the BBC again. They always put it "another way", ie the Tory way, twisting and lying about everything I say.

Shall we forget about spoons?

Oh, so we're *not* talking about spoons suddenly. Typical BBC. You're obviously working for them. Oh, yes, it all makes sense now. You were born with a silver spoon in your mouth, like everyone at the BBC... what a disgrace.

I know this is purely hypothetical, but has anything amusing ever happened to you in connection with a spoon?

No. But I expect the BBC will make up some story about me and a spoon. What a disgrace they are.

NEXT WEEK: *Sir Thomas Legg: 'Me And My Leg'.*

Opera Highlights
Rigelouto
by Berlusconi

Act One

THE curtain rises on the balcony of the Palazzo Legova where the Robber Baron is having an important breakfast meeting with a number of young female members of the European parliament.

He is however dismayed to find an angry crowd of citizens has gathered to demonstrate against him. They sing the chorus **Silvio Bastardo Corrupto!** *(Nobody should be above the law).*

Horrified by this display of disloyalty Silvio entreats them to remember his good works and particularly his generosity to the young women of the town. He sings the aria **Mille e Tre** *(I have taken a purely professional interest in over a thousand of them).*

Act Two

We are in the highest court in the land and a chorus of 15 learned judges are considering the Robber Baron's case. His lawyers, Cartero and Fucci sing **Tutti Immuni Silvio** *(My client is guilty but there is nothing you can do about it).* The judges, however, decide that Silvio is not above the law and sing **Tutti Egali in Legia** *(You're nicked, matey)* and tell him that he must stand trial for fraud, bribing a judge, tax evasion, associating with courtesans, frequenting with minors and bringing the office of the Robber Baron into disrepute.

Act Three

To everyone's surprise, Silvio is undaunted. He explains that under Italian law no-one over 70 can go to jail. He sings **Sono Settanta Tre** *(I am 98).* He then holds a party in the bedroom of the palazzo and invites all the village maidens to share in his good fortune. They all sing **Viva Silvio! Viva Espagna!** *(surely 'Italia'? Ed.)*

"Singing is all I've ever really wanted to do"

From The Message Boards

Members of the online community respond to the major issues of the day...

Newcastle police order drunks to clean up their own mess

The officers did no more than make the street-foulers right their wrongs. Inasmuch and insofar as they did so do, then, as Isaiah taught, they did no more than the men to whom Rabshakeh was sent, who did no more than eat their own dung and drink their own piss. – *Mr_Salmon*

This follows my proposal that the armed forces should urinate on war memorials with dignified discipline and make the yobs lick them clean. Now here's another idea. The law allows any pregnant woman to urinate anywhere at any time. SUCH IS THE STATUS WE ACCORD MOTHERHOOD. What better way of showing our contempt for the yobs than to organise a taskforce of law-abiding ladies with child? They could urinate on the streets and ORDER the yobs to lick the pavements clean. Any yobs lying unconscious would be urinated upon and they could lick themselves clean when they finally awaken. The ladies would relieve themselves with pride and the yobs would get a taste of their own medicine. – *Public_Spirited_Citizen*

its sea monky sea monky do 🙄 they shuld sit an example like in saudi wen they chopd the head off the pedo an put his body on public displey 💀 lets hav 3 strike's an ur out FIRST a fence get down on hand's and nee's an scrub up the wee with a two'thbrush then brush there teeth with it 😊 secund a fence no two'thbrush just lick it up 😋 thirde a fence OFF WITH THERE HEAD'S an put the body's in the street 😆 THEY WONT DO THAT AGAIN IN A HURY – *Broken_Britan*

Beautifully put, Broken. As victims' champion Sara Payne MBE says, the punishment must fit the crime. – *Rot_in_hell_Myra*

sara payne this sara payne that its all me me me 😡 no mention of maddie in sarahs law 😡 lazy cow dint even think up a difrent name 4 her owne little girls name 😡 scum 😡 rip with the angle's little sarah y did u die an not ur mum – *Justice_4_Maddie*

That Honorary Degree Citation In Full

SALUTAMUS JACOBUS DEE COMICUS MISERABILIS ET NOVUS HOSTUS 'REGRETTO, NON HABEO CLUEDO!' IN RADIO IV QUONDAM ALCOHOLICUS NON-EMPLOYMENS IN DEPRESSIONE ET CETERA ET CETERA SED NUNC FAMOSISSIMA PER COMEDIA ERECTA E.G. 'VIVENS AB APPOLLO' QUOQUE SCRIPTIT LIBER BIOGRAPHIENS CELEBRITATIO PER FESTIVALE CHRISTUS NATUS APPELATUS "GRATI PER NULLI" (REDUCTIO AB £VII.IC IN OMNIA TABERNA BONA) GAUDETE (SED NON JACOBUS QUIS NON RIDIT SEMPER)! GEDDIT? LAUDAMUS DEE-O ! GEDDIT ?

© The University of Winchester (formerly King Alfred's Catering College), Hants.

POETRY CORNER

**In Memoriam
Tom Fleming**

So. Farewell
Then
Tom Fleming.

Solemn-voiced BBC
Commentator on
State occasions.

Yes, we remember
You particularly at
Royal funerals.

But who
Will commentate
On yours?

E.J. Thribbute
(17½ gun salute)

**In Memoriam
Chris Haney, inventor of
Trivial Pursuit**

So. Farewell
Then
Chris Haney.

Inventor of
Trivial Pursuit.

It would make
A very good
Question.

"What was the name
Of the man who
Invented
Trivial Pursuit?"

No one
Would know
The answer.

E.J. Thribb (17½)

**In Memoriam
Harry Carpenter, TV's
'Voice of Boxing'**

So. Farewell
Then
Harry Carpenter.
TV's 'Voice of Boxing'.

'The Rumble in the Jungle'.
That was your
Greatest moment.

1,2,3,4,5,6,7,8,9...
TEN!
Yes, you have been counted
Out.

E.J. Thribb (17½ stone)

DIARY

PAUL JOHNSON

ALBERT EINSTEIN (1879-1955) knew nothing worth knowing about physics. But he did know a lot about cooking.

He was a master at cauliflower cheese. But I have never liked cauliflower cheese. Too cauliflowery, too cheesey.

I prefer roast beef. But Albert was no good at roast beef. He overcooked it.

He was always asking me for advice on relativity. I told him it was a complicated and foolish business, not worth the fuss about. But he persisted because he always loved the media attention.

It did for him in the end. Today, Albert is barely remembered outside the pages of the specialist magazines.

MARILYN MONROE (1926-1962) had no sex appeal. But she was desperate to get on. Sometimes I would find myself sitting next to her at the Beefsteak Club. No-one else would touch her with a barge pole. She was dowdy in the worst sense of the word.

She was always grateful for my beauty advice. But it was an uphill struggle. She was a bad listener.

"Men never like a woman who shows too much cleavage and pouts" I explained. "If I were you, I'd wear a long skirt in brown or beige. Stop colouring your hair. And stop speaking in that silly way."

I once introduced her to Noel Coward, a well-known womaniser. He showed no interest in her.

No-one remembers Marilyn any more. Her films, such as they were, are never watched.

SHERLOCK HOLMES (1865-1928) was not nearly so clever as his brother Mycroft, who I knew well. Sherlock considered himself a big cheese but he never solved a case worth mentioning. Men who smoke pipes make poor detectives. Their attention is always on the pipe, never on the case.

WINSTON CHURCHILL (1874-1965) was always pestering me for advice, even though I was only a child. He was desperately unsure of himself. I had been the first to alert him about Adolf Hitler. Winston took him for a charmer but I told him he was up to no good. "Never trust a man with a side-parting" I warned, "He'll always try to put one over one you."

And so it proved. But Winston got the better of Adolf in the end. On VE Day, he collared me in the Savoy. "Ay oop lad. You were right about Hitler" he conceded in his broad Lancashire accent.

PRINCESS DIANA (1961-1997) had a stubborn streak. She would never take no for an answer, even when I insisted I was married. She was the most intelligent woman I ever met, fascinated by everything I said. She died in a car crash in Rome. They say she was holding a copy of one of my books, I forget which.

MAHATMA GANDHI (1869-1948): was much fatter than he looked. He used to wear a baggy loincloth, size XL, to cover up his great big belly. He was the fattest man I ever knew.

He was notoriously pugnacious. A quick jab from Mahatma and you'd be on the floor, begging for mercy. He disapproved of boxing-gloves, saying they were for sissies.

What made him so aggressive? I put it down to all that meat he ate. "You should eat more fruit and veg, Mahatma" I told him.

He wore funny little spectacles. They did nothing for his image. I told him to buy something more manly, with proper horn-rims. He failed to do so and he was assassinated.

He came from India, but knew nothing of its people or traditions. But he knew all the words to *My Old Man's A Dustman*. His favourite colour was navy blue.

BUGS BUNNY (1938-1963) cut a ludicrous figure. He had big ears and protuberant teeth and generally went around with nothing on. He often had a carrot in his hand. He affected a lisp. I used to meet him at Kingsley Martin's flat and later at J.B. Priestley's.

He once sought my advice. "There are three rules for a great rabbit" I said. "Never show off. Don't act the giddy-goat. And if you must go into the movies, make sure you only go after the serious roles."

MUHAMMAD ALI (1942-) made a name for himself as a boxer. We met briefly. He was well built. I found him receptive to good advice. I taught him how to improve his game. "Stop dancing around. Concentrate. Act like a man. And remember to punch." It did the trick.

He had dark skin, which led some to mistake him for a negro.

REGINALD KRAY (1933-2000) had the finest manners of any person I ever knew. A typical Balliol man. He would always stand up when a woman entered the room, unless she was ugly or had fat ankles. A lot of gossip has been spread about his involvement in crime. Stuff and nonsense. He was the finest Christian I ever knew, apart from Pope John Paul II, who wasn't English. Reggie always remembered to say his prayers, particularly when there was a dead body in the room.

As told to CRAIG BROWN

THE DAILY STAR ★

HEROD SEEKS COMPENSATION OVER BABY J CASE

by Beth Lee Hemm

The controversial figure at the centre of the Baby J case is suing over what he calls his "unfair treatment".

King Herod was widely condemned at the time for his failure to prevent all the firstborn in the land being slaughtered. But Herod's lawyer, Keith Shekel, last night claimed that Herod has been victimised as a result of a "public outcry whipped up by the Bible."

Unstable

"My client did nothing wrong. He followed all the standard procedures which are laid down for authorities to implement in the event of the birth of a Messiah. All the boxes were ticked, but regrettably all the babies were murdered."

Mr Shekel continued, "In fact, Herod deserves a pay rise on account

of the fact that Baby J survived the so-called Massacre of the Innocents and his upbringing has been successful after his placement with his stepfather and single mother.

Bad Tidings

Herod is demanding substantial compensation of "Gold, Frankincense and Myrrh" to recompense him for the very considerable stress involved in his "successful handling of this very complex case".

On other pages
- Three for Two offer on Wise Men **p.2**
- Pret-Away-in-a-Manger Turkey Sandwich offer **p.3**
- Royal David's Citybreaks **p.4**

An Apology

LAST MONTH our distinguished football correspondent E.I. Adios may have given readers the impression that England had already won the World Cup. Headlines such as 'England Win World Cup!', 'England Win World Cup!' and 'World Cup Won By England!' may have led readers to believe that the national football team were in some way in contention to win the coveted World Cup trophy.

We now realise, following a 1-0 defeat by the Ukraine, that the current England side is the worst group of footballers ever assembled by an England manager in the entire history of the game. This sad truth is conveyed in our more recent headlines – 'Capello Must Die!', 'String Up Rio!' and 'Bring Back Sven!'

We apologise for any confusion caused by this unfortunate misunderstanding, which we promise not to repeat until the next time England win.

"We find we're saving a lot of money during this recession by regurgitating food"

QUESTION TIME SHOCK

Yes, you sir... the gentleman at the back in the brown shirt

WHY ARE THE BBC GIVING THE BNP ALL THIS FREE PUBLICITY?

★ See Pages 1-94

PLUS Pics, Letters, Supplements, Comment, Leaders, Blog etc. etc.

'Should BBC be allowed on airwaves?'

● The question the nation is asking

MARK THOMPSON, leader of the notorious BBC, was last night at the centre of a growing storm over allowing its highly controversial views to be broadcast.

Thompson heads an organisation with thousands of members, many of whose views are deeply offensive to the vast majority of the British public.

One fierce opponent of the BBC's right to continue broadcasting its "odious propaganda" is Sussex landowner, Charles Moore.

Last night he told us "These people pretend to be sensible, balanced normal individuals, but we know that, beneath the surface, they are just foul-mouthed bullies and thugs, who go round attacking old age pensioners on their answerphones."

No Sacks Please – We're British National Party

But from his headquarters at the aptly named 'White' City, Thompson hit back at his critics saying, "We have every right to be on television, because we are hugely popular all over the country. We are the only organisation which addresses the concerns of ordinary people – ballroom dancing, antique-collecting and snooker."

What do you think?
Should the BBC be kept off the air?

☐ Yes ☐ No ☐ They should all be sent home

ME AND MY SPOON

THIS WEEK

NICK GRIFFIN

Where do your spoons come from?

I am proud to say that, like Winston Churchill, I possess only British spoons. The import of non-indigenous spoons has done nothing but debase the purity of the spoon-base.

You said in 1983 that you hated black spoons and that you wouldn't ever have one in the house.

Er... I was misquoted... I never actually said that... You're just trying to make me look like Hitler.

Talking of which, you are on record in 1993 as being an admirer of Hitler's pamphlet 'Mein Spoon'.

No, that's not right, I never said that.

I've got the quote here. You said, "Adolf is a very great leader and collector of pure Aryan spoons".

No, no I didn't. And under European Law I can't say anymore or else I'll be prosecuted as a spoon-hater. The majority of ordinary men and women in this country believe as I do that we've got to stop these foreign spoons coming in and filling our cutlery drawers forcing out...

I'afraid that's all we've got time for. I'm not going to ask you if anything amusing has ever happened to you in connection with a spoon because you're a Nazi.

– ❖ –

The editor of *Me and My Spoon* writes in defence of his controversial decision to invite the BNP leader to take part in *Me and My Spoon*

In a democratic society we had no alternative but to invite an elected BNP representative to talk about spoons. Failure to do so would have been an attack on free speech and could well have resulted in a fall in our circulation. Not that I have looked at the figures, but our readership has now gone up to 8 million following Mr Griffin's appearance. Which proves my decision was correct.

On Other Pages

● Should we have given a platform to the Editor of the Spoon Column to defend his decision to invite Nick Griffin to talk about Spoons? **p1**
● How did Griffin perform Spoon-wise? You give your opinion on the BNP leader's answers. **p2**
● What our celebrity panel thought about Griffin on Spoons. A A Gill, Sir Alex Ferguson, Gordon Ramsay, Graham Norton and Cheryl Cole give their verdict on the biggest night in Spoon history. **p3**

TV celeb Nick Griffin does Hole In The Wall

Great Military Operations
No. 94 The Surge of the Light Brigade

We'll go into the Valley of Death, having set a firm deadline for retreat...

Great Figures From Oriental History No. 94

Salman The Magnificent

THERE lived in those days a very wealthy nobleman who had amassed great treasures from the sale of his scrolls, which were circulated throughout Christendom and also Muslimdom.

Indeed, so fearful were the Ayatollahs of the Islamic lands that they decreed that his scrolls should be burned and that Salman should be put to death.

But Salman prevailed against all his foes and defied the fearsome clerics of the East by producing even more scrolls, which filled the scroll shops of the West even though, as the ancient jesters joked, these literary offerings "failed to ignite".

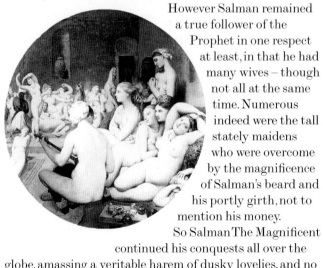

However Salman remained a true follower of the Prophet in one respect at least, in that he had many wives – though not all at the same time. Numerous indeed were the tall stately maidens who were overcome by the magnificence of Salman's beard and his portly girth, not to mention his money.

So Salman The Magnificent continued his conquests all over the globe, amassing a veritable harem of dusky lovelies, and no longer spent his days toiling at his scrolls, so great was the prowess of this Passionate Potentate of the Pen.

© Translated from the Arabic by Lunchtime O'MarKhayyam

BBC'S NIGHT OF SHAME –
Why Aren't They Wearing Poppies?

by Phil Buttonhole

YOU'D think the BBC would have learned their lesson – but no, yet again they have offended the whole country.

The deliberate snub by the meerkats on David Attenborough's "Life" programme is an insult to our war heroes living and dead.

In the very week that we remember the fallen, the meerkats blatantly spit on the graves of our servicemen and women by refusing to wear poppies when appearing on air.

Last night there were calls for the meerkats to be sacked and their excessive salaries to be drastically reduced.

Said one outraged Daily Mail reporter, "This is typical of the left-wing, liberal, anti-British Broadcasting Corporation, which should be broken up and the profitable parts sold to Lord Rothermere."

WORLD UPROAR FORCES SLAGG TO APOLOGISE

by Our Media Staff **Lunchtime O'Boyzone**

AN ARTICLE by Eye columnist Glenda Slagg on the subject of Seamus Gayfeller, a late member of the popular Dublin-based singing group Bogzone, has drawn over two million complaints to the Press Complaints Commission, the Race Relations Board and the UN Security Council.

A campaign on the social networking site Twitter called for Ms Slagg to be tried for war crimes and for the death penalty to be restored in this particular case.

Moir Means Worse

Faced with the threat of prosecution under the Prevention of Terrorism Act 2008, Ms Slagg issued a clarification through her lawyers.

"OK, so I said he was a sleazy poof. Who cares? What sort of world are we living in where you can't call someone a sleazy poof?"

The paper's editor explained, "Ms Slagg is keen to make it clear that she deeply regrets any offence she may have caused to our advertisers who are threatening to cancel their contracts, and wishes to assure readers that her comments were not meant to be in any way homophobic."

GLENDA'S CONTROVERSIAL COLUMN LAST WEEK

■ SEAMUS GAYFELLER!?!! Who did he think he was, a-mincin' and a-wincin', a preenin' and a queenin', with his boyfriend (sorry, Mr PC, 'civil partner'). No wonder the gay brigade all end up dead when they behave like Shameless (geddit?)

Did you want to kill Glenda when you read the article? Text now to Gagtheslaggdailymail.co.uk

GLENDA'S COLUMN TODAY

■ SPARE A THOUGHT for poor Seamus Gayfeller, the gifted musician who sadly... (cont. p.94)

St Cakes Headmaster Calls 'For National Debate On Education'

BY OUR SCHOOL STAFF
MICHAEL WHITEBOARD

The headmaster of St Cakes School, the prestigious Midlands Independent School, motto: "Quis Paget Entrat", Mr Anthony Kipling, M.A., has called for a country-wide debate about the future of our children's education.

He told reporters, "Far too many of today's headmasters spend their time running their schools when they could be engaged in writing biographies of the Prime Minister, organising national debates on education or giving interviews to the Telegraph such as this one."

Mr Kipling was speaking at the launch of his latest book, "The Happiness Curriculum: How You Can Be Happy by Being A Famous Headmaster" *(Seldon Press £19.99).*

National Treasure Island

Cluff

MONTY PYTHON'S FAMOUS DEAD HORSE SKETCH IN FULL

(Bookshop. Enter customer, who addresses shop assistant.)

John Cleese: *(points to pile of Python anniversary books)* Hello, my good man. I wish to register a complaint. This horse that you are trying to flog me is dead! You are flogging a dead horse!

Michael Palin: No, there's plenty of life in it. Book, CD, DVD, TV documentary…

John Cleese: It is an ex-horse! It has ceased to be! It has shuffled off its mortal coil and joined the choir invisible!

Michael Palin: No, it's not. It's a live stage show at the Royal Albert Hall.

John Cleese: It's a stiff! If it weren't for the fact that some of us have divorces to pay for, it would be six feet under and *(continued for next 94 years)*.

POLICE LOG

Neasden Central Police Station

0833 hrs Armed SWAT team of 12 officers called out to incident at Mary Seacole Primary School in Lidl Road in response to emergency call from Lee Asbo, aged 8½.

0852 hrs Officers arrive at crime scene to discover suspect, geography teacher Derek Mapp, 63, explaining action of volcanoes to Year 4.

0903 hrs Under rigorous interrogation involving low-level Taser deployment (94,000 volts) Mapp admits verbal abuse of pupil – i.e. telling Asbo to "stop eating crisps and concentrate".

0917 hrs Mother of victim, Chantelle Asbo and live-in partner, Steve Lager arrive to be briefed about "horrific abuse of their son".

0925 hrs Mapp charged with Aggravated Assault, Attempted Homicide and Crimes Against Humanity.

1011 hrs Suspect arrives at Neasden Police Station.

1012 hrs Body of suspect taken to Neasden Mortuary.

1027 hrs Coroner's report on the late Mr Mapp finds "accidental death by Swine Flu".

Notes&queries

What is 'string theory'?

(Mrs Stephanie Hawking, Cambridge)

● "String theory" was first developed in the 1930s at Battenburg University by Professor Hans Twining, who argued that the entire universe was made, not from atoms as had been previously thought, but from particles of string. His famous paper "Das Univers von Stringpartikel Gemacht" (1933) was supressed by Hitler as a "Jewish Conspiracy". The theory was revived in the 1980s by a team of mathematicians at Berkeley, California, led by Professor Melvin R. Ropey. It was briefly known as "Ropey Theory" before reverting to its original title as "String Theory" and is now generally accepted as the most plausible explanation for the structure and nature of the universe.
Rev. A.K.H. Reef-Knot

What is the origin of the now popular expression "dissing"?

● Contrary to the explanation offered by Sir Vidia Naipaul, the word is not a patois abbreviation for the term "disrespecting". In fact, it goes back to the 17th Century and was derived from the Norfolk market town of Diss, the inhabitants of which were well known for their puritanical zealotry. Outsiders who came to the town and behaved "immodestly or intemperately" were subjected to long moral lectures and were even put in the stocks. This was known as being given "a good Dissing" (as was recorded by Daniel Defoe in his celebrated *Tour of the British Isles*).
Dr Horace Saumarez-Smith, archivist of the Norfolk Museum of the Rural Environment, Diss

Is it true that ants can't walk backwards?

● Not this old chestnut again! I thought we'd laid this to rest decades ago. How many more times do I have to point out what should be obvious to anyone who has studied ant behaviour – that these insects only walk forwards? The still unfortunately widespread misconception that ants can "retro-ambulate" comes from a celebrated April Fool hoax perpetrated by the BBC's Natural History Unit in 1957, which depended on the simple trick of reversing the film. I hope that I will not have to write again on this subject, since I see from my files that I have already done so 67 times and I have many better things to do with my time.
Cedric Formica-Smith, Beddington

Answers please to the following:

Did Leonardo invent the internet? Do fish cause global warming? Is Sir David Frost still alive?

TV Highlights

Still available on the BBC iPlayer
Imagine on Scrabble BBC1

ALAN YENTOB looks at the fascinating history of the world's most famous word game and discovers that 'Botney' is the highest scoring word that can be used in a scrabble competition.

'Botney' (which means "a hirsute multi-tasking executive – from the Persian 'Beardie') earns you up to 389,000 pounds (surely 'points'? Ed.) and automatically qualifies you for a treble bonus score.

Less popular, according to Yentob, is the word 'Bragg' (meaning floppy-haired rival arts supremo – from the Cumbrian 'Bargg').

"Mirrorball, mirrorball on the ceiling, who dances best to 'sexual healing'?"

That Cameron Conference Speech In Full

I WANT to get straight to the point. Yes, things are terrible. Yes, there is a steep climb, but when we get to the top we will be able to throw ourselves off. And may I just have a standing ovation at this point for mentioning the armed forces and their brave leader, General Dannatt, who has risked everything to join the Conservative Party. *(Standing ovation)*

I am a simple person. I believe in Family, Community and Country. And in my wife. May I have another standing ovation for saying how much I love her, even though I did not get her to introduce me like the cynical Gordon Brown. *(Standing ovation)*

We must pay off our debts. My debt in particular is to Tony Blair. So can I just say things

that the conference does not usually support, but say them in a rising cadence that means you applaud wildly at the end? The NHS, women candidates, civil partnerships, the NHS, devolution, the environment, fighting poverty, the NHS, higher taxes, financial regulation, the NHS, international aid and the NHS? *(Standing ovation)*

Let me read out some emails. That is what they do on the radio when they can't think of anything to say between songs. And yes, *Reasons To Be Cheerful* is a great song that is coming up next. But first, the weather. *(Standing ovation)*

Everything is the fault of Big Government doing too much. Especially the banking crisis where the government did too little. Er... time to read out some more emails from poor people. *(Standing ovation)*

Finally, I know that all our promises to cut spending and freeze pay are very depressing. But remember our record of breaking promises and you'll suddenly feel a whole lot better. And now *Reason to Believe* by the Arctic Monkeys. *(Final standing ovation lasting 94 minutes)*

Formerly 'Drawing All Faiths Together', Now 'Doing Anything For Tesco'

To the Prime Minister of Israel

Dear Mr Netanyahu (or may I call you Benjamin?),

I'm sorry I haven't been in touch for a while over the peace process business, but I have been kept rather busy elsewhere in the world, as you may have noticed!

First, they wanted me to be the President of Europe, then I had to help out my colleagues at J. P. Morgan by attending a prayer meeting in New York, and finally I had a very important engagement in China, speaking at the Shanghai Retail Businesswoman Of The Year Regional Awards Lunch (truly it is said that a great man's work is never done – and in my case that is very, very true!).

But now to more serious matters. I have been approached by a good friend who has come up with a very imaginative proposal for bringing the two communities in your country closer together. The great advantage of his idea is that it offers thousands of jobs and is entirely self-financing.

We have an ideal site in mind for this project in Jerusalem, which is central and open to access by members of all the main local faith groups.

May I present to you the "Dome of The Rock Tesco" (open seven days a week, except Friday and Saturday, which, as you know, Benny, are holy days!).

To allay any security fears, there will be a very substantial barrier or wall built down the centre of the retail space, thus ensuring that those purchasing matzos and chicken soup will not be inconvenienced by having to mingle with those customers asking for their land back (surely for "Own-Brand Halal Meal For Two" Ed.).

This visionary business opportunity from Tesco, I am sure you will agree, Ben old friend, deserves your full and earnest consideration, as a step forward to bringing together myself with a lot of money. (Is this right? Ed.)

Shalom,

Rev. T. Blair
Chief Executive, D.A.F.T.
(former vicar of St. El Albion's)

WILL THE TWO NO-HOPERS PULL OFF AN UNLIKELY VICTORY?

by Our Political Staff **Jedward Sturton**

They have silly hair! They're annoying! They're irritating! And neither has a shred of talent.

Yet the whole country is talking about them.

Can Gordon Brown and Alistair Darling go on and win the next election?

"We admire their thick skin and tenacity," said X Factor twins John and Edward Grimes. "If we'd have had some of the terrible things people say to them said to us, we'd be in pieces. Good luck to them."

"A victory for talentless nonentities like Brown and Darling would be a disaster and put young talent off entering British politics for life," moaned Simon Cowell.

It's Deadwood!
(Surely 'Jedward'? Ed.)

● *Do you think the plucky underdogs can win it??*

Then phone our special Gnome 'ZZZ Factor' phone line (calls charged at £18 a minute. Minutes last 18 seconds).

TELEVISION ROYALTY

Jedward & Mrs Simpson

U.N. 'DESPERATE TO AVERT CRISIS'

by Our Showbiz Staff **Russell Tweet**

THE U.N. security council met last night in emergency session in an attempt to broker a peace deal between Stephen Fry and Twitter.

"The whole world has been rocked by the news that Stephen Fry might leave Twitter because someone was slightly rude to him," said the U.N. Secretary-General Ban Ki-moon, "this is surely the greatest crisis the world has even known, and will ever know for all eternity."

Predictions that stock markets would plunge, and hundreds of millions of people would be left homeless as a result, thankfully proved unfounded when a few hours later Stephen Fry apologised for his "hissy fit" and resumed tweeting once again

about his "having a cup of tea" *(cont. 94 times a day)*

● Meanwhile, celebrities everywhere were devastated at the news that an ordinary member of the public had used the internet to call Stephen Fry "dull".

"I would never have guessed that people were using such highly derogatory words such as 'dull' when discussing celebrities on the internet," said a horrified Britney Spears. "I certainly hope no one has ever been as abusive as that about me on the net."

"I always assumed the internet was a lovely, kind, forgiving, gentle place," added a crestfallen Lindsay Lohan, "but if people are using horrible words like 'dull' on it, then obviously I must be wrong." *(cont. p. 94)*

'GIVING ADVICE' MORE DANGEROUS THAN RIDING A HORSE

by Our Medical Staff **Dr L.S. Dee**

OFFERING advice on drug classification to government ministers is more dangerous than going out for a ride on a horse, Professor Nutt warned today.

"The facts speak for themselves. Very few people who indulge in equestrian pursuits are sacked by Alan Johnson," he said, "whereas my research shows that 100% of those suggesting changes to the narcotics classification system are summarily dismissed and told their careers are dead.

"So the message is clear," he concluded. "Kids! Don't get addicted to science. You'll become a scientific adviser in no time and after that you'll end up jobless in the gutter."

Daily Mail
COMMENT

Of Course Professor Nuttcase Must Be Sacked

FOR once, Alan Johnson has got something right. If a so-called drugs expert goes round telling toddlers and teenagers that to go out and get stoned on ecstasy and weed is better for their health than falling off a horse after a couple of glasses of wine, then it's a no-brainer.

This potty professor has become a major danger to the health of everyone in these islands. The only advice we would all like to offer him is to "get nutted".

On other pages: Letters supporting our point of view from 15 professors of psychiatry, pharmacology, neurology, etc.

theguardian

Of course Professor Nutt-Guilty should be reinstated

If anyone should be sacked, it's Alan Johnson, for his arrogant refusal to listen to genuine science in the person of the highly-respected Professor Nutt.

How typical of this high-handed politician to imagine that he knows better than one of the most distinguished scientists in the country.

When Professor Nutt analyses the dangers of moderate cannabis and ecstasy usage, comparing them with the proven risks of such extreme sports as horse-riding or opening a bottle of Chardonnay, he deserves to be listened to with proper attention.

The only honourable course left to the Home Secretary is to resign forthwith and admit that he is the real "nut".

On other pages: Letters supporting our point of view from 15 professors of psychiatry, pharmacology and neurology.

"Mum, can I have a book in my room?"

UPROAR GREETS NEW MP RULES

by Our Political Staff **Peter O'Bore**

WESTMINSTER erupted in fury last night when Sir Christopher Kelly unveiled his shock new proposals for curbing MPs' abuse of their allowances system.

Said Sir Christopher, "I hope this will mark the beginning of a new era, when our politicians again regain the trust and respect of the nation."

But MPs were quick to condemn Kelly's recommendations as "jolly unfair, outrageous, absurdly draconian, and in many ways far worse than Hitler's Germany."

THOSE PROPOSALS IN FULL

HOUSING

MPs will in future be allowed no more than three homes, only one of which may be used as a love-nest for recreational purposes, or as a temporary hostel for illegal immigrants.

FAMILY MEMBERS

MPs will no longer be permitted to employ their wives, children, parents or civil partners in any capacity whatsoever, whether secretarial, managerial

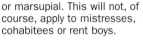

or marsupial. This will not, of course, apply to mistresses, cohabitees or rent boys.

FOOD AND DRINK

MPs will not be allowed to claim overnight subsistence allowances of more than £2,000 per meal, not to include any wines more agreeable than Jacob Rees-Mogg's Creek Somerset Shiraz (£599).

TROUSER PRESS

MPs staying in an ordinary 5-star hotel while on parliamentary business shall only be permitted to claim for hire of a trouser press for no more than 20 minutes.

Kelly's final recommendation was that "the nation's desire to see a wholesale crackdown on the wasting of public money should be met by the setting-up of a new supervisory body, IPSA (the Inordinate Parliamentary Spending Authority), to be headed by the distinguished lawyer, Sir Ian Kennedy, who cannot be expected to take on such an onerous and responsible task for a salary of less than £500,000 p.a. for a three-day lunch (*Surely 'three-day week'? Ed*).

"He's standing down at the next election"

1O DOWNING STREET
LONDON SW1A 2AA

Draft Speech for Justification of War

~~2004~~ 2009

We cannot just cut and run. Our troops are in ~~Iraq~~ Afghanistan for the foreseeable future. They will stay for as long as the ~~Iraqi~~ Afghan government needs them. They are the front line in the fight against terrorism and if we were to withdraw from ~~Iraq~~ Afghanistan there would be civil war between the various ~~Iraqi~~ Afghan factions and a return to lawlessness.

To sound a retreat without completing our mission to bring stable democracy to ~~Iraq~~ Afghanistan would send a strong message to ~~al Quaeda~~ the Taliban that they had achieved a victory. The sad but inevitable recent losses in ~~Basra~~ Helmand only reinforce our determination to see the job through.

~~T. Blair~~ G. Brown

Memo to MoD: Prepare for retreat. Suggest date in ~~2007~~ 2010 please – if possible before election. Thank you.

ON OTHER PAGES From the Archives: Why we must never let the Russians win. There must be no retreat from Crimea – 1854

What You Missed

The Today Programme
Radio 4

Evan Davis (*for it is he*): Good morning, Lord Mandelson. Thank you for coming on the programme.

Lord Mandelson (*for it is he*): Hullo, sailor!

Davis: Get you!

Mandy: Aren't you going to ask me one of your naughty questions?

Davis: Cheeky!

Mandy: Ooh, hark at her!

A fuller version of this interview on the government's legislative programme is available on our website at todaytrash/bbc/slash/slash/don'tbotherit'stoo complicated.

DUNCAN SPEAKS OUT OVER EXPENSES

We deeply regret our behaviour over expenses

ME AND MY SPOON

THIS WEEK

ANDREW MARR

Can I first of all ask you...

No, I'm afraid that it's a private matter and there's an outstanding injunction on this column.

May I then...

No, I'm afraid you are not allowed to even mention that there is an injunction.

Can we then talk about other people's spoons?

Certainly. They are very interesting. I mean, the things politicians get up to with their spoons. Gordon Brown, David Cameron. It's scandalous, I tell you.

Can we turn back to your spoons...

No, you'll be hearing from my solicitors.

Thank you.

NEXT WEEK: *Keith Schilling – "Me And My Shillings".*

That Honorary Degree Citation In Full

SALUTAMUS DAVIDUM PARADINUM FROSTICUM, TELEVISIONIS PERSONALITATEM LONGEVITISSIMUS (AETATE CVII). PRIMO SATIRISTUS ANNO DOMINI CMMLXII CELEBRATUS QUAM PRESENTOR "HOC ERAT SEPTEM DIES HOC ERAT" (ANNO DOMINI CMMLXII) CUM MILLICENTIA MARTINA ET GULIELMO RUSHTONE DIRECTUS AB NEDDO TWINKIO (AKA SHERRINO) BENE COGNATUS CUM OMNIBUS POPULIS PER CATCHUS PHRASUS "SALVE, BONUS VESPERUS ET AVE" TUNC, QUAM MAGNUS INQUISITOR, INTERROGAVIT MULTOS CELEBRITATES PER EXEMPLO HAROLDO WISLONE ET EMILIO SAVUNDRA, CROOKUS TREMENDICUS. SED CLIMACTICUS EXTRAORDINARIUS ERAT SUO CONFRONTATIONE CUM RICARDO NIXONE, EX-PRESIDENTE AMERICANO POST SCANDALE "AQUAPORTA" (SUBSEQUENTER TRANSLATUS IN TEATRO SPECTACULO ET BLOCKBUSTERENSIS CINEMATOGRAPHICUS "FROSTUM NIXONUM"). NUNC DISMISSUS AB BBC RETIRAVIT AD AL JAZEERAM, CANALIS ARABICUM OBSCURANTICUS. TRISTIS FINALIS AD CAREERUM GLITTERENSIS. VALE, BONUS NOCTUS, ET GAUDEAMUS.

© The University of Winchester (formerly The M3 Polytechnic)

Bryony Gordon
Fleet Street's Most Controversial Columnist

Dog mess on the pavements – I know you're not meant to say this, but I hate it! Why can't dog owners just pick it up? Here's a suggestion that will have the PC brigade foaming at the mouth – pop the poo in a plastic bag and put it in a bin! I'm sorry if I've upset anyone but it's what I think.

☐ The Second World War – OK, shoot me down in flames, but I happen to think that Britain was on the right side.

Sorry if you're a Nazi, but British troops fought for the freedom of columnists like me to state the truth – however uncomfortable it may be. So I'll say it again. I'm personally *glad* that Adolf Hitler was defeated.

☐ I love Cheryl Cole – there, I've said it. I know no-one else does and its going to annoy millions of you out there – but I've never been afraid to fly in the face of public opinion. Whatever anyone else may think, *I'm* sticking to my guns – Cheryl Cole is very pretty and quite sweet. And you can send me all the hate mail you like, it won't change my mind!

(This is dynamite. More please, Bryony. "Thirsty" W.L.)

Issued by the Scottish Tourist Office

SPOT THE BALLS

"I'm not a bully...   ...and anyone who says I am...   ...is going to get their head kicked in"

"We're very lucky, really, with our poltergeist"

POLLY FILLER

I'M in full agreement with the educational experts who say it's absurd that children in Britain start school at the age of four! It's insane! Mad! Plain old-fashioned bonkers! They should start school at the age of two! If not earlier!

What's even more crackers is the nutty professor's recommendation that kids start school at six! That's S-I-X! Can you believe it?

Six in the morning maybe – but six years old? Every mother's nightmare!

Clearly, the loony who thought up this hare-brained scheme is a man – because it's nothing less than an attack on working women.

By which I mean, of course, the au pair (Pau Pah from riot-torn Xing Jiang, since you ask!).

How on earth is the silly girl going to combine childcare, laundry, cleaning, gardening, cooking and supermarket shopping (not to mention renewing the TV licence and taking the car for its MOT) with having an energetic toddler under her feet all day? Impossible!

IT's disgraceful and unfair. Looking after a gifted infant like Charlie is a full-time job and if Pau Pah has to supervise him walking the hamster – and it's not as though she'll have any help from the Useless Simon who is too busy playing Poker On-line in the hope of virtually meeting Victoria Coren... how sad is that Simon? It's never going to happen, do you hear? Never!... anyway, where was I?

Oh yes, school starting age. If Professor Egghead-Interfering-Busybody wants Charlie to wait until he's six before he goes to school then perhaps he would like to come round Chez Filler and spend his empty day taking Charlie to see "Up" for the seventh time!! Because some of us women have got jobs to do (get on with the ironing, Pau Pah!) and others have got columns to write!!

© P. Filler 2009.

23

The Alternative Rocky Horror Service Book

No. 94 A Memorial Service to Commemorate the Life of a Famous and Devout Atheist

The President: A very warm welcome indeed to all our brothers and sisters from the media who have come here to this place of worship in order to take pictures of you all for tomorrow's newspapers. May I begin by asking all the celebrities present to stand up and give a sign to the photographers.

Here Shall Follow the Taking of the Photographs

The President: We are gathered here today to give thanks for the life of *(here he may say Sir John Mortimer or Sir Ludovic Kennedy or some other famous non-believer)*. Obviously, we are not giving thanks to God, because none of you believe in all that nonsense *(laughter)*.

So shall we start with a famous reading by a famous actor. *(Here he may say Jeremy Irons, Stephen Fry, Judi Dench or someone similar)*.

Reading from the Book of Ecclesiasticus

"Let us now praise famous personalities, men (and of course women) renowned for their celebrity; such as those who appeared regularly on TV and were frequently interviewed in the newspapers. All these were honoured with knighthoods and CBEs."

The President: That's enough of the reading. Now it is time for some music played by some of the famous friends of the famous celebrity whose memory we are honouring today in this beautiful old cathedral, which is available for hire at a very reasonable rate for such occasions as corporate dinners, book launches and editions of the Antiques Roadshow.

(The music which shall follow may be rock 'n' roll, jazz, songs from the shows, Frank Sinatra or any other popular style of music, so long as it is not a hymn.)

Prayers

The President: There will be no prayers.

The Creed

All Shall Here Say: We don't believe in God the Father Almighty, although we are prepared to concede that Jesus had many good points. We believe in basic human values as exemplified in the life of the late N or M – laughter, fine wine, the company of attractive women and agreeable holidays in Tuscany.

Here They May Also Say: We also believe in the basic human right to assisted suicide with the assistance of the Dignitas clinic in Switzerland, because there is no afterlife, obviously.

The President: So that's pretty well it. It's been a really fun occasion and I almost forgot we were in a church! *(Here the congregation may laugh)*. As N or M once wittily remarked to the Sunday Times, "Going to church is the last thing I shall ever do." *(Here they may laugh again)*

The Dismissal

The President: You may now all go out for more photographs and interviews on the church steps especially for any mistresses and love-children.

The Blessing

Vicar: Bless!

All: Bless!

Vicar: Bless.

All: We mustn't come more often!

(The congregation shall then leave to a suitable piece of music, it may be the Trumpet Voluntary Euthanasia by Jeremiah Clarkson or the theme from What the Papers Say [trad.])

Those Vatican Summit Talks In Full

Very Reverend Rowan Atkinson: Perhaps we could begin by focusing on the need for our two faith communities to try to establish a framework for moving forward towards a possible situation in which both churches feel comfortable working together to create a constructive relationship which could both embrace our respective traditions and yet...

His Holiness Benedict XCIV: Gott in Himmel! For you, Beardie, ze Church is over! Auf wiedersehen schweinhund!

"I find that symbol of your faith offensive and want you sacked from your job"

IMAGINE: Yentob Meets Bassey

Hey, big spender!

Leave my expenses out of it

"We constantly monitor your BBC transmissions, so naturally we thought this was how you dressed"

New Words
with Philip Howard

Aspiration, noun. Political target known to be unachievable but promised anyway. Example: "When I said I would abolish the congestion charge, this was an aspiration," Mayor of London, 2009.

Inquiry, noun. Semi-legal process involving taking notes and making statements which can later be filed and forgotten about – e.g. Hutton Inquiry, Butler Inquiry, Chilcot Inquiry.

Underperforming, adj. Euphemistic term for NHS hospital found to be unsatisfactory. Synonym for "Highly dangerous, toxic, lethal".

IRAQ INQUIRY – DAY 94
'AMERICANS WERE GHASTLY,' CHILCOT TOLD

THE INQUIRY into the Iraq War yesterday heard evidence from Sir Mandarin Orange, the former private secretary to the private secretary to the Cabinet.

"Our American friends had very little idea of what they were doing," said Sir Mandarin.

"Very early on we told them that we knew all about how to handle these terrorist chaps because we'd done it before in Northern Ireland.

"But these frightful Americans didn't listen to us. No wonder it all went completely pear-shaped."

Meyer Culpa

The inquiry then heard from Sir Christopher Satsuma, former Ambassador to Washington, who said that he had written several times to the Prime Minister Tony Blair, telling him not to trust President Bush who, in his words, was "pretty ghastly" and "frightful".

"Now that Blair is out of power," Sir Christopher went on, "I can speak freely. I can tell you that I never rated him very highly, and incidentally all this is in my book *'Blair Was A Bastard'*, which is now on sale in all good bookshops".

The inquiry then heard from Sir Hector Tangerine, the former Deputy Head of MI6, who explained "We all knew that Saddam had no weapons of mass-destruction, but we thought that in the circumstances it would be much better not to tell anyone."

The inquiry continues.

WHITE HOUSE GATE-CRASHERS EXPOSED

by Our American Staff **Boy George Washington**

AN UNKNOWN British couple pulled off a daring coup, it has been revealed, by managing to gatecrash a party thrown by the President of the United States, Barack Obama.

They even had themselves photographed alongside the President and the First Lady, who chatted with them as if they were legitimate guests.

Watergatecrashers

"It was amazing," said Londoner Gordon Brown. "We got past the security and no one once questioned who we were.

"We had drinks and canapes and everything," went on his socialite wife Sarah. "They were really friendly and the President asked Gordon whether we were enjoying our time in America, before moving on to chat with a man who owns a potato farm in Idaho."

Red-faced FBI chiefs last night apologised for the severe security lapse, which had allowed two complete outsiders to get near to the President.

Gatecrashing bore

"It was a major blooper," said one senior White House protection officer. "This guy turned out to be a real loony-toon – thinks he's a Prime Minister or something. He even talks about having a 'special relationship' with the President – this is some dumb kook, I tell you."

● Full story and pics p. 94

Great Tales of Chivalry No. 94
Sir Boris and the Oiks

AND IT happened in those days in the streets of London that a young and innocent maiden was being beaten up by some even younger maidens. And she cried out for help. "Help, help!" she cried. But there was no one to come to her aid.

Then suddenly she heard the tinkling of a bicycle bell and in the darkness a manly voice called out, "Cripes, what's going on here?"

And the maiden replied, "My prayers have been answered. You are my knight in a shiny plastic helmet!"

"Clear off, you oiks!", said Sir Boris, as he dismounted from his trusty bicycle and waved his umbrella at the iron-bar-wielding miscreants.

"Gosh, it is Sir Boris!" cried the maiden, as the oikettes fled in terror from the frowning mien of the gallant knight.

"I confess that I voted for Sir Ken, the Red Knight," she spake coyly, "but now I realise that in a fight you really need Sir Boris."

And, with danger past, the very parfit gentle knight even offered to take the maiden home on the back of his bicycle.

But, knowing of his reputation, she graciously replied, "No, thank you, kind sir, I think I'll walk."

But Sir Boris was glad in his heart to have performed such an act of chivalry, saying to himself, "Blimey, Sir Dave back at Cameronlot will be jolly batey when he reads about this in the *Daily Telegraph*."

Jonathan Ross gets an answerphone message from Andrew Sachs

25

RECORD LOTTERY WINNERS 'THRILLED' BY BUMPER PAY-OUT

*by Our Economics Staff **Jack Pot***

THE British winners of the biggest ever single pay-out came forward yesterday to claim their multi-million pound jackpot.

The two luckiest men in Britain are both coincidentally senior executives of leading British banks, Sir Phil Boots of the Royal Bank of Scotland and Sir Ivor Bonus of Lloyds TSB.

They each made an initial modest outlay of 0p and were rewarded by an incredible return of £90 billion each.

Officials at the National Lottery (HM Treasury) had initially been surprised when no-one came forward to collect their winnings, but it emerged that both men had been on extended holidays – Sir Phil on his yacht, "The Jolly Rich", and Sir Ivor on his yacht, "The Jolly Rich II".

Looking tanned and fat, Sir Phil told reporters, "I cannot believe my good fortune. When Mr Darling rang me with the good news I thought he was joking. But no, the giant cheque is mine."

Completely Bankers

Asked how he would spend the money Sir Phil said, "I'm certainly not going to put it in a bank. That would be madness. No, I will give some to worthy causes such as my colleagues' bonuses and the rest I shall invest in champagne, cigars and other luxury items."

Sir Ivor added, "This will not change my life. I have always been extremely rich and quite unpleasant and I intend to carry on this way."

Notes&queries

I have read in the paper that the Manchester United footballer Wayne Rooney has named his newly-born son 'Kai'. Do any readers know the origin of this unusual nomenclature?

(Rev. Mandy Hassock-Smith, E. Sussex)

● "Kai" is the ancient Egyptian word for 'swan", an animal which was believed to be sacred, on account of its rarity in the Nile Delta. The swan-headed god Kai-Roo can be seen in the burial chamber of the Pharaoh King Tutiphusupportas (Late to Middle Kingdom 2094-5094 BC).
Dr. Ryan O'Spearmint, Professor of Egyptology, Waterford University, Co. Durham

● Dr O'Spearmint could not be further from the truth. Kai (which is pronounced to rhyme with Pi) is the highest in a range of inaccessible mountains in Northern Japan, discovered in 1328 by the celebrated Japanese Explorer Ho Su Kai after whom the peak was named.
Sir Nicholas Tobasco, FRCS, Travellers Club

● What a lot of bollocks! These two supposedly learned gentlemen need to get out more. Anyone with kiddies knows there is a brilliant computer game called Death Judgement 7 in which the ninja assassin who does battle with the army of zombie killer ants is called *Kai*!! It is obvious to me that Wayne is a Death Judgement 7 aficionado and has probably, whilst assuming the avatar "Kai", amassed, as I have, over 7 million zombie ant "kills".
Ron Gazza, London Cab No. 7742358

(PS. I should like to take this opportunity to wish Wayne, Colleen and baby Kai good health and happiness in years to come.)

Answers please to the following:

What makes rain wet?
Did Hitler play the banjo?
What is Lembit Opik's real name?

'I Was Bel de Mooney,' Admits Daily Mail Columnist

*by **Rowan Pelling**, former editor of 'The Erratic Review'*

FOR YEARS her identity was one of the most closely guarded secrets in Fleet Street.

Millions of readers hung on her every word, as she confessed to her secret life "writing for money".

By day, Bel de Looney was a respectable Somerset divorcee and yurt dweller, formerly married to a leading TV personality, who she says, "knew nothing of what I was getting up to when I was out of the house".

Her West Country neighbours knew her as "Mrs Dimbleby", as she drove around in her 4x4, promoting green causes.

Belle de Jour-nalist

None of them suspected that she was, in fact, the notorious Mail columnist Bel de Mooney, paid hundreds of thousands of pounds by a reclusive "Mr Big" (Paul Dacre), who would dictate exactly what she was meant to write.

Bel herself was unrepentant when her pseudonym was uncovered.

"In the modern world," she said, "women are free to do anything they want, and if that includes writing highly intimate pieces about their personal life in return for large cheques, so be it."

On Other Pages

● "Is £300 an hour too much for being a Daily Mail regular?" by Janet Street-Walker **94**

● "Why oh why is she being paid more than me?" asks A.N. Wilson **95**

● "Why Bel de Mooney is wrong to glamourise the dark world of writing for the Daily Mail," writes Mel de Phillips **96**

● "What's wrong with enjoying Christmas shopping?" demands Sir Max Hastings **97**

PLUS Your Trains Tonight – Bel de Brighton (cancelled)

Judge Hits Back At Press Critics

by Our Legal Staff **JOSHUA ROSENBERG**

A SENIOR High Court Judge, Mr Justice Cockleady, last night hit out at journalists who dared to criticise his role in a number of recent high-profile libel actions.

"Any suggestion that I am in some way biased against the press," said the judge, "is a disgraceful slur which I consider to be tantamount to the offence of criminal libel, or *scandalum magnatum*, to give it its full legal nomenclature.

"Any journalist who is in any way guilty of being personally abusive of myself shall be taken from this court and hanged by the neck until he has apologised."

Mr Justice Eady is 106.

God! It's like everyone I've ever slept with is here.

CHILDREN'S CLASSICS UPDATED

The Tiger Who Came to Tee

One day a Tiger came to tee. Then he shagged everything that moved until his wife found out and he didn't come to tee again.

Fwore!

I didn't sleep with Tiger Woods!!!

GOSH!!! WOW!!! COR!!!

UK GOLD
Columbo – Episode 94
The Case Of The Gentlemen's Club

(Silly music. Luxurious residence in downtown Florida. Shabby car draws up outside and man in raincoat with cigar climbs out and rings bell)

Butler: Can I help you, sir?

Columbo: I am Lieutenant Columbo of the Los Angeles Police Department. *(Surely Florida? Ed.)* I was hoping to speak to Mr Woods.

Butler: You and a million others, sir.

(Cut to palatial interior with marble pillars and Rembrandts on the wall. The world's most famous golfer is practising his putting on the carpet)

Columbo: Say, this is quite a place you got here, sir. And may I ask where you got this carpet? You know, Mrs Columbo is a great admirer of your game. She watches all your tournaments on TV.

Woods: Is there some point to this, Lieutenant? I am a very busy man, trying to avoid talking to the police.

Columbo: It's just when I came in, sir, I couldn't help noticing the car in the drive. It looks all smashed up, as though the driver had hit a fire hydrant. Have you any explanation for that, sir?

Woods: There could be any number of explanations. The driver could have been under a lot of stress.

Columbo *(slaps forehead)*: That's it, sir, obviously. Stress! Now it begins to make sense. *(Relights cigar and prepares to leave)* Oh, there's just

one more thing, sir...

Woods: Yes?

Columbo: The back window of the car... it looks as though a woman smashed it in with a golf club. Maybe it was his wife after an argument about a nightclub hostess or something... That's a beautiful picture, sir. Is it your wife? Or maybe it's your girlfriend...?

Woods: You'd better have something to back that up, Columbo, or you'll be looking for a new job. I think you should leave.

Columbo: I'm sorry, sir. I was just leaving. I think I've got everything I want.

(Columbo leaves room. Woods sighs with relief and begins to phone girlfriend. Columbo re-enters)

Columbo: Just one more thing...

(Woods breaks down in tears)

Woods: I confess... I have transgressed... I have sinned against my family... But, Lieutenant, how on earth did you find out?

Columbo: I read it all in the newspapers, sir, and very interesting it was too.

(Silly music. Titles. End)

WOODS TAKES BREAK

NEWS was emerging last night that Tiger Woods is planning to take what has been described as an "indefinite break" from extra-marital affairs for the foreseeable future.

A spokesman for Mr Woods said, "For the past decade, Tiger has been focused on becoming the world's number one philanderer, something which has put an immense strain on his relationship with those he holds most dear – namely Gillette, TAG Heuer and Nike".

On Other Pages

● **Media Don't Take Break From Tiger Woods Story**

DEFINING AZERBAIJANI FAIR TRADE
(formerly Drawing All Faiths Together)

Hello!

And there's only one thing on the global agenda this week – Formaldehyde! Yes, it's not something people talk about a lot nowadays – but hey, people are wrong with a capital W!!

I was recently privileged to be invited by President Baadman of Azerbaijan – one of the good guys! – to open a fantastic new state of the art formaldehyde factory in the beautiful unspoilt countryside just outside Szhithol on the banks of the River Poizzon – which the President tells me is the Riviera of tomorrow!. And look I'm not going to disagree with him – especially not now I've got my cheque for 50 million gromits and a free lifetime supply of formaldehyde!!!

My old friend, Cherie, once said to me, "Vicar, you can never have too much money or formaldehyde." And hey, isn't that something for us all to think about in this season of Advent/Eid/Diwali/Yuletide/Thetan Festival of the Second Coming of L. Ron Hubbard? Apart of course from thinking about formaldehyde!

Yours
Rev. T. Blair
Chief Executive, D.A.F.T.
(former vicar of St. Albion's)

POETRY CORNER

In Memoriam Richard Todd, Film Star And Real-Life War Hero

So. Farewell
Then
Richard Todd.

Star of *The Dambusters*.

You played Guy
Gibson VC.

"Steady. Steady.
Steady. Down
A little. Steady.
NOW!"

Yes. That was
Your catchphrase.

In the film
You had a
Black Labrador
Which we
Had better call
Nigel.

And what
About your
Theme tune?
All together now –
Da da da da
Diddy dum dum da...

      E.J. Thribb (17½)

In Memoriam Maggie Jones – acid-tongued battleaxe Blanche in Coronation Street (Deirdre's mother and Ken Barlow's mother-in-law)

So. Farewell
Then Maggie
Jones.

Acid-tongued Battleaxe
Blanche
In *Coronation Street*,
(Deirdre's mother
And Ken Barlow's
Mother-in-law).

Now, like so many
Others in the cast,
You have made your
Last exit.

But the show goes on.
For ever.

      E.J. Thribb (17½)

Scenes You Seldom See

"My wife and I were wondering – could you play some Lady Gaga?"

"The State pension is more than enough. I even manage to put a bit away each week"

"This is all very personal, Andrew. I have no intention of discussing it on my mobile in public"

In Memoriam Kim Peek, Idiot Savant and Inspiration for The Rain Man

So. Farewell
Then Kim Peek.

Given a date,
You could
Say what day
Of the week
It was
In seconds.

For example: October
13th 1729 –
"It was a
Tuesday,"
You would say.

You have now
Passed on.

On December 19th, 2009.
It was
A Saturday.

      E.J. Thribb (17½)

In Memoriam Bill McLaren, Rugby Commentator

So. Farewell
Then Bill
McLaren.

You were the voice
Of rugby.

With your deep
Scottish brogue
You enriched us all
Even if we
Couldn't always
Understand you.

"And there'll
Be dancing
In the streets
Of Auchtermuchty
Tonight."

That was your
Catchphrase.

But sadly there'll be
No dancing
In the streets
Of Auchtermuchty
Tonight.

      E.J. Thribb (17½–nil)

TV THIS WEEK

BBC1 8pm Monday

Her Majesty

ZOE PRITCHETT plays the young Queen Elizabeth in furious conflict with Sir Winston Churchill (Miles Price) over the Mau Mau uprising. "I don't believe I'm hearing this," she tells the famous wartime premier.

BBC4 9pm Tuesday

Barbara

LOTTY WORSLEY plays the young Barbara Cartland and the author's darker side is revealed as we see her torrid affair with playwright Noel Coward (Mark Eastman). "You're doing my head in, Noely," she tells him.

Channel 4 10pm Wednesday

Myra

CAITLIN MACNAMARA plays the legendary concert pianist Dame Myra Hess as she battles with her demons of depression and drug addiction following the break up of her tragic relationship with ukulele star George Formby (Bradley Wilson). "I need some space, Myra ducks, for some me-time," George tells the distraught Myra.

BBC3 11.00pm Thursday

Margaret

EMILY KEITHLEY-STRIBBS plays the young Margaret Rutherford as the fledgling actress embarks on a lesbian relationship with Dame Agatha Christie (played by Enid Blyton). When Agatha cruelly rejects Margaret, the young Princess Elizabeth (Myra Hindley) intervenes to comfort her and asks Sir Winston Churchill (Noel Coward) to postpone his plans for World War Two. "Maggie, Maggie, Maggie. Come out, come out, come out," he tells Stalin.

(That's enough terrible biopics, Ed.)

PM APOLOGISES FOR AUSTRALIAN MIGRANT TRAGEDY

by Our Apologies Staff **Mia Culpa**

GORDON BROWN spoke tonight of his "intense sadness" at the revelation that little Ben Elton had been sent off to Australia.

Mr Brown wept openly before the TV cameras as he admitted that the British government had pursued a heartless policy of driving out very rich comedy stars by taxing them at 50%.

Furthermore, the international best-seller novelist and musical librettist was under the impression that he would enjoy a much happier life Down Under, living with wallabies and kangaroos who would laugh at his jokes.

"The truth was," sad Mr Brown, "we were desperate to get rid of little Ben because we were sick of him droning on about how much he hated Britain, how awful the Queen was, and how ungrateful the Brtitish public were for all that he had done for them."

Mr Brown said he was "deeply sorry" to the Australians for sending them Mr Elton, in what he described as "one of the most shameful episodes in British history".

The Australian prime minister last night hit back by apologising to the British people for sending them a flood of unwanted migrants. He named Germaine Greer, Clive James, Rolf Harris and Kathy Lette as examples of *(cont. p. 94)*

Gospel According to St Matthew (Parris)

(MODERNISED VERSION)

THE STORY OF ZACCHAEUS

1 And there was a rich young man called Zacchaeus, who was known as Zac. And he yearned to become a faithful follower of the Promised Messiah, that was David, son of Cameron.

2 And Zac went up into a tree, to show how Green he was, to await the coming of his leader.

3 But then Zac was sore troubled, for he remembereth that he was a non-dom, which in his language meaneth one who avoideth paying taxes.

4 However, David cometh to the tree and shouteth up, "Zac, Zac, come down from the tree, for I haveth a solution to the problem of you being a tax avoider.

5 "I tell you it is easier for a rich man to get into Parliament if he remaineth in the country and payeth his taxes."

6 And Zac jumpeth down from the tree, crying out, "Whatever thou sayest is right, Dave – we Etonites must stick together."

7 And they went on their way rejoicing.

ME AND MY SPOON

SALLY BERCOW

As the Speaker's wife do you have a large collection of spoons in your official residence?

Yes it's true, I spent a lot of my early days getting legless. I liked to drink buckets. So what?

I'm sorry, how do spoons come into this exactly?

And when I was really drunk I would go to bed with anyone who bought me a drink. I was a real slapper, I suppose you'd say.

Could we get back to the subject of spoons? You must do a great deal of entertaining as the Speaker's wife?

Oh, all right, there were drugs as well – weed mostly. I don't remember to be honest, I was so out of it…

So, er, do you have a favourite spoon?

If I'm going to be a Labour MP and stop the evil Tories getting into power, I've got to be really honest and open.

So, has anything amusing ever happened to you in connection with a spoon?

I'm afraid I can't talk about that, it's a private matter. *(Pause)*. Did I tell you about the bloke dressed up as a chicken? God, I was drunk that night.

I'm afraid that's all we have time for.

NEXT WEEK: *Katherine Rake, of the Family Parenting Institute, "Me And My Rake".*

WE'LL MEET AGAIN DON'T KNOW WHERE...

29

DIARY

SARAH BROWN

I'm a "people person" – and I'm not ashamed to admit it!

I'm often reading about people who've really "done their bit" for others less well off than they are – and I really think these heroes are worth celebrating! So, here goes! What follows is a list of people – some of them personal friends, others role models we might all hope to emulate – who truly struggled to "make a difference". I salute them!

NORMAN BATES

Yes, I've heard all the scurrilous gossip that puts it about he's in some way a bit of a "psycho", but, hey, guys, let's not listen to the rumour machine. The Norman Bates I know – who, incidentally, has done some brilliant catering for us at Number 10 – is a real softie, kind, diligent and with a heart of pure gold. And Norman dearly loves his old mum, who's clearly quite a character: on top of running his own motel, Norman is always popping up to see her. He has this profound sense of duty, coupled with social justice and a great conscience.

PIERS MORGAN

If anyone can make me giggle, it's Piers! The guy's so cheeky! I call him the Oscar Wilde de nos jours, always ready with a hilarious – and often outrageous! – "quip". And he makes Gordon chuckle too! He's not one to kow-tow to those in power – no, he says just what he thinks – even if it's to the Prime Minister! For instance, the other day he came round to dinner and he said to Gordon, "You may be a bit of a plonker, Gordon – but, seriously, you're the only guy with the brilliance and integrity to run this country, and I'm with you all the way!" Yes, Piers is fearless – and that's why he's my hero!

GOLIATH

They say he was a giant and a Philistine, but in my experience Goliath was a real sweetie. If he was a giant, he was a gentle giant, and as for him being a Philistine, well, take it from me, he did a great deal of unsung behind-the-scenes work for the ballet. As for David, for all I know he may have been a perfectly nice person but is it really fair and socially just to take a sling and five stones in with you when you go into battle? I'm sorry but no, that's not what I call fair or just or decent. Goliath was the real anti-establishment candidate. We in the West have so much to learn from him.

DAMIAN McBRIDE and CHARLIE WHELAN

Please don't ask me to choose between them – because I love 'em both dearly! One or two politically-motivated critics who simply probably never even met this smashing pair of "cheeky chappies" have accused them of being "tough" or "fearless in their defence of the Prime Minister". Please could someone tell me what's so very wrong with that? Damian and Charlie are a lot of laughs and as loyal as the day is long. Why shouldn't those who think it's fair game to attack the Prime Minister when he's doing his level best to run this country expect a bit of a "talking-to" from the boys? OK, sometimes they may go "too far", but I wish people would have a sense of humour about it, and, anyway, when has "going too far" ever been a crime?

PARIS HILTON

Nothing about her public image prepares you for the first meeting with Paris. Turns out she's a smart, caring, considerate person and deeply intelligent, with a genuine love of ordinary people and a whole-hearted belief in caring for those less fortunate than herself.

NURSE MILDRED RATCHED

It's a tough, tough job caring for folk with mental health issues, so three cheers for Nurse Ratched, who did such truly brilliant work at the Salem, Oregon Mental Hospital for so many years. Mildred is now living in retirement, but she remains indefatigable, and still finds time to drop into Number 10 to offer us her valuable advice on caring for the unstable, the troublesome and those who are in any other way not quite "on-line". Mildred is a great believer in the soothing power of medicine, and I've noticed that Gordon is always a lot calmer after one of her visits!

NAOMI CAMPBELL

The Naomi Campbell I had heard about was beautiful, successful, always late, a bit frightening, even a bit out of control. The Naomi Campbell I met was certainly beautiful, but also generous, authentic and impatient in a good way. The Naomi I know hates to see injustice and inequality. That's why she orders people about, in a good way, and keeps people waiting, in a good way. If she screams and shouts at underdogs it's only in a good way, because she's a fearless challenger of the established position and her profound sense of social equality prevents her from thinking of them as overdogs.

MR KURTZ

A far cry from his ever-so-grumpy press image, Mr Kurtz is warm, tremendous fun, loves people and gets a real kick out of helping others, especially those from ethnic minorities.

GORDON BROWN

What can I say? He's fun. He's carefree. He's patient. He hasn't got a grudge in the world. He's Gordon. And he's my big teddy bear.

As told to CRAIG BROWN

BBC Radio 3

Opera Latest
The Punchback of Notre Duomo

by Berlusconi

Act One

THE Robber Baron is staging a huge party in one of his many palaces, to celebrate all his achievements over the past year. He sings **Sono tutti fabuloso** (*I am the most handsome man in Italy*).

The crowd applauds wildly, singing the chorus **Te amore Silvio** (*We can't wait for your fourth term*).

The indefatigable Silvio then bares his chest to the assembled courtesans and dancing girls who are admiringly thronging round him and sings the aria **No vesti la giubba** (*See, I am so tough that I do not wear a vest*).

Act Two

The Robber Baron's display of hubris swiftly brings an unexpected nemesis. The village idiot breaks through the throng singing the taunting aria **Where is Silvio, who is he?** (cleverly borrowed from Schubert). In an act heavy with symbolism, he hits Silvio over the head with a life-size model of the Milan Cathedral. The crowd gasps in horror, as Silvio falls blooded to the floor.

The chorus mournfully sings **La commedia è finita** (*Looks like the party's over*).

Act Three

The curtain rises on an empty square. A lone news vendor enters, singing the sensational headline **Il trionfo di Silvio**. It transpires that, following the assault, the Baron has soared in popularity. In fact, he has never been so loved by his people.

Silvio is then wheeled on in his hospital bed, surrounded by a chorus of semi-naked nurses, and sings **All I want for Christmas is my two front teeth**. As festal bells ring out, everyone joins in with the closing chorus: **Tutte che voglio per Natale e i miei due denti frontale**.

A Government Apology

IN RECENT months we may have given the mistaken impression that the Al Qaeda terror threat originated from Afghanistan and that was the reason why tens of thousands of British troops have been deployed to fight in Helmand province.

We now realise, in the wake of the attempt to blow up a Delta airliner, that nothing could be further from the truth, and that the terror threat from Al Qaeda comes in fact from Yemen.

We apologise to those killed and injured in Afghanistan and also to those who will be killed and injured in Yemen when America invades it next year.

FORTY YEARS OF THE *SUN*

How Britain's Favourite Newspaper Chronicled The Events That Shaped The World

BBC COVERAGE USELESS

Man lands on Moon, 1969

GOTCHA! BBC CAUGHT SUPPORTING ARGIES

Falklands War, 1982

'BBC ATE MY HAMSTER' – Freddie Starr's Shock Claim

Celebrity madness, 1986

WHY HASN'T THE BBC COLLAPSED AS WELL?

Berlin Wall falls, 1989

HOORAH FOR SKY TV!

First Gulf War, 1990

BBC MURDERS PEOPLE'S PRINCESS – OFFICIAL

Death of Diana, 1997

BBC IN EXPENSES SCANDAL

MPs' expenses scandal, 2009

TIME TO CLOSE DOWN THE BBC AND GIVE THE BEST BITS TO MR MURDOCH!

...and what we can look forward to when the Queen dies

The Alternative Rocky Horror Service Book

No. 94 New African Liturgy for the Summary Execution of Homosexuals.

Bishop Onanugu (for it is he): We are gathered here to administer the holy sacrament of Execution to our brother N'__ or M'__.

All: String him up! (Or they may say, "Hanging is too good for him").

Onanugu: Who casteth the first stone?

Congregation: We do.

(There shall then be a Reading from the Book of the Black Cabbie [Kampala Cabs No. 1274] vs. 1-3)

Reader: No, don't get me wrong, guv, I've got nothing against them, but let's face it, they should all die. I 'ad that Peter Tatchell in the back of the cab once. He was lucky to get out alive.

All: Thanks be to God.

(The congregation shall then sing Hymn no. 94 "The Gay Though Gavest Lord Has Ended")

The Peace

(Here the congregation shall give each other a sign of peace)

Onanugu: Nothing too friendly, boys, or I might start to think you are a bunch of shirtlifters and you'll wind up on the end of my rope!

All: Point taken, boss.

The Dismissal

(The congregation will dismiss the views of the Archbishop of Canterbury by the ancient act of voodoo, according to the extreme rites of the Anglican Church of Christ Witch Doctor)

Onanugu: You may now come forward and stick pins in this effigy of the Right Reverend Rowan Willliams.

All: Take that, Beardie!

(The congregation will then process out of the church to the place of execution)

Onanugu: Happy Christmas to you all!

Storm Grows as Leader Refuses to Renounce Nuclear Ambitions

by London Staff **Our Man In A Dinner Jacket**

THE increasingly deranged British leader, the Ayatollah Gordoni, yesterday stepped up his plans for his country to maintain an independent nuclear capability, despite strong pressure from Iran and the increasing doubts of his own people at home.

Gordoni, however, is adamant that Britain's Trident missiles are only there for peaceful purposes, and that Britain has no desire to threaten its neighbours.

The hugely expensive nuclear programme is fast bankrupting the country, whose students have already taken to the streets to do their Christmas shopping.

In addition, workers in the key aviation industry are threatening to go on strike through the period of the religious festival known as Xmas, when Britain's millions of devout agnostics traditionally get drunk, eat turkeys and watch television.

DANISH CARTOONIST SHOCK

I suggested a link between Islam and violence

Let's kill him!

☙ ANCIENT TIMES ❧

WORLD'S TALLEST STRUCTURE OPENED IN DESERT

by Our Architectural Staff **Percy 'Burj' Shelley**

Antique Land, Thursday

THERE WAS great excitement today as the world's biggest statue was unveiled. Hundreds of travellers witnessed the opening ceremony of the tallest ever monument, a triumph of engineering built on the lone and level sands and dedicated

to the mighty local ruler Ozymandias.

"This vast edifice will stand for ever," the King of Kings told reporters, "and it certainly won't fall down and become a metaphor for vanity and folly... hang on... watch out... run for your lives..."

ROW GROWS OVER MEDAL 'HOAX' CLAIM

by **William GeorgeCross**

VETERANS today queried the bona fides of a man seen sporting a row of medals to which he was "not entitled" at a Remembrance Day parade.

The veterans' suspicions were aroused when the man in question, calling himself only "Prince Charles", was caught wearing all of the following medals: the Grand Order of King Leopold of the Belgians (1st class); the Star of the Siege of Leningrad; the McDonalds' Employee of the Week; the Campaign Medal for the Battle of Hastings; the Purple Heart (Korea) and the Blue Peter Badge (1972).

When confronted, the Prince said that he was in the SAS and therefore bound by the Official Secrets Act.

Queen's Schilling

He added that his war record was a private matter and he would be instructing his solicitors, Messrs Carter and Ruck, to prevent any further discussion of the matter.

"Who left the top off the toothpaste?"

NEW LAW TO ALLOW WORLD LEADERS TO VISIT BRITAIN SAFELY

by Our Legal Correspondent **Joshua Rosenbeard**

MPs expressed outrage last night over an emergency Bill proposed by the government which will make it impossible for visiting world statesmen to face arrest for war crimes when they enter Britain.

The issue has arisen following attempts by pressure groups to indict Mr Tony Blair, a former British prime minister, when he recently made one of his rare visits to Britain.

Livni And Let Livni

Alan Milbank, Chairman of the UK Friends of Blair group, last night said, "It is outrageous that someone of Tony's standing in the world cannot even come here to make an after dinner speech to a group of local Rotarians for a token fee of £2 million without the threat of being put into prison as a major war criminal.

Missy Tzipi

"It is absurd to call Tony a war criminal just because he invaded Iraq for no good reason, resulting in the deaths of a million innocent people. Why, next you will be saying that the Israelis were up to no good when they killed all those people in Gaza." *(Cont. p. 94)*

The Romance of the Century
When Love Beckons

by Lady Antonia Fraser (as told to award-winning authoress Dame Sylvie Krin)

THE STORY SO FAR: Harold and Antonia were unlikely lovers. He, a rough diamond from the slums of Finchley. She, a blue-blooded bluestocking from the salons of Inverness And yet, at that fateful dinner party in Mayfair, a spark between them ignited a fire that would burn brightly for over half a century. Now read on...

THERE was a long pause. Then finally Harold spoke. "You're not fucking going, are you chummy?"

Lady Antonia blushed as she stood holding her mink fur cape, framed in the doorway in the moonlight. She struggled for an answer to his romantic entreaty. Her heart was saying, "Yes, yes, yes", but another voice was counselling "What about your husband, your children, your elderly father, the social reformer and anti-pornography campaigner, Lord Longford?".

And then there was Harold's wife

Vivian, the beautiful actress... No, no, it was too terrible to contemplate!

And yet, as she turned and stared into the limpid pools of Harold's deep, dark magnetic eyes in their horn-rimmed spectacles, she hesitated.

"Make your fucking mind up, sweetheart," he growled.

And with those words, Lady Antonia knew she could not resist her destiny. A great avalanche of love engulfed her and she was lost. *(To be continued...)*

Answers to Eye Quiz

1. Odd Man Out
The answer is (d) Peter Tatchell, all the others have beards.

2. Who Said What?
(a) The Duke of Edinburgh; (b) Victoria Beckham; (c) Dame Judi Dench; (d) Sir Fred Goodwin.

3. Who Gets There First?
The answer is Mr B. If he starts his journey at 8.30 and walks due north to the bus station at 3mph, he will arrive in time to catch the 10.15, meaning that he will arrive in Darlington four-and-a-half minutes before Mr A, who walked due east for 12 miles. Meanwhile Mr D attempted to cycle on the snowbound section of the M27, which had been left ungritted and so failed to reach his destination.

4. Robert Peston's unusual way of talking is not a deliberate affectation. It is due to a rare medical condition known as acute emphasytis, which means that the sufferer cannot avoid placing the emphasis on the wrong syllable of every word he utters. So the answer is (d).

Picture Quiz

(a) Velázquez – *Las Paedophilias*;
(b) Rembrandt – *Portrait of the Artist as an Old Man*; (c) Vermeer – *Girl With An iPod*;
(d) Van Gogh – *Sun Glasses*; (e) Banksy – *Adoration of the Magi*.

Letter to the Editor
Names of the year

Sir, As is my custom, I send you a list of the most popular names given to children born in the last year, based on the birth announcements column of your esteemed newspaper:

Boys	Girls
1. Avatar	Subo
2. Jedward	Cheryl
3. Tiger	Jade
4. Lidl	Alisha
5. Drogba	Annunziata
6. Jacko	Asda
7. Abdulmutallab	Obesia
8. Izzard	Nutella
9. Triffid	Triffidia
10. Mr Justice Eady	Lady Antonia Fraser

CANON TEABAG
MONTEFIORE-TOBLERONE,
The Old Nuclear Power Station, Berks.

POLLY FILLER

I TELL you what – being snowed in proved to be absolutely marvellous for the Filler household! Time stopped as Nature gave us a welcome pause to consider all the things that really matter in life and that we forget all too easily in our rushed, busy, high-stress lives.

Instead, we Fillers were forced to stop the clocks and enjoy the simple wintry pleasures – becoming children once again in our joy of snowball fights, tobogganing, building snowmen and going for long walks in the winter wonderland.

Sadly, I had this column to write, so I couldn't join in the fun and my partner, the useless Simon, was holed up watching *James May Builds A 100 Foot Model of Top Gear's Richard Hammond Out Of Airfix Spitfire Kits* on Dave Plus Gold Again!

SO, our hopeless new au pair, Goo Gul from China, had the blissful task of looking after toddler Charlie on her own – and nearly ruined everything by complaining about the cold and retreating indoors to play Wii Tobogganing with him!

Do you know, I was almost sorry when the snow finally melted, particularly when I realised that I couldn't get another column out of it next week!

© All newspapers.

"Looks like the wintry weather is losing its appeal for him"

COUNCILS DEFEND GRITTING RECORD

by Our Weather Staff **Jack Frost** and **Peter Snow**

AS TRAVEL chaos continued to sweep Britain's ice-bound roads, local councils have hit back at criticism of their performance by members of the public.

Said one senior official, Councillor Slipshod, "What people don't understand is that the roads are very icy. We can't send gritting lorries out in those sort of conditions because it would be very dangerous."

He continued, "The lorries might career off the road and crash – then we wouldn't have any gritters at all. Is that what the public wants? I think not."

Ice work

He concluded, "The safest option is clearly to keep the gritters indoors until weather conditions improve and there is no need for them any more."

THE DAILY TELEGRAPH

Letters *to the Editor*

The Great Freeze

SIR – To those who remember the winter of 1947, the recent mild cold snap bears no comparison whatsoever to the months of Siberian conditions which lasted from well before Christmas to the end of May.

As a small boy at St Cakes prep-school, I vividly recall how even our unheated dormitories were under six feet of snow. We were ordered by our headmaster, Rev Aloysius Kipling (affectionately known to all the boys as 'Kippers'), to break up our benches and desks to be used to fuel the school boiler.

For months we survived only on a diet of raw swedes and tinned beetroot, shrewdly stockpiled by the Bursar, Major Mosley, for just such an eventuality.

But was the school closed down by these "adverse weather conditions", as so many have been in these present spineless and health-and-safety-conscious times?

Not a bit of it. We even managed to improvise a ski-slope on the Chapel roof, which gave hours of innocent pleasure to us 12-year-olds, only two or three of whom plummeted to their deaths, to be commemorated in a plaque in the chancel to this day.
Sir Herbert Gusset,
The Old Gritting Shed,
Lymeswold-under-Snow,
Staffs.

SIR – I am fed up with hearing your younger readers reminiscing about the so-called "Winter of 1947". To those of us who came through the truly awesome winter of 1926, 1947 was a mere bagatelle.

As a schoolboy at St Biscuit's preparatory school, I vividly remember (cont. p. 94)

Daily Mail

SNOW. Isn't it wonderful? That's all Britain's been going on about as the countryside turns into a winter wonderland.

Well, all I can say is "What tommy-rot!"

There's only one good thing about snow – and that is that it turns into slush!

Just say the word out loud. And don't you get a sense of that wonderful feeling when you stride down your drive into the lane, kicking up the lovely grey slush in all directions!

So what if it soaks your trouser bottoms and leaks into your Hunters?

Isn't that all part of the fun of good honest British slush?

**Great stuff.
Keep going. Ed.**

You can keep your beastly snow and your rotten icicles, let alone your babyish tobogganing and your boring snowmen.

The only good thing about a snowman is when it starts to melt and turns into – guess what? –

Why I Love Slush

by the **World's Worst Columnist MAX HASTINGS**

fabulous irresistible SLUSH!

Speaking for myself, I can't get enough of slush – which is why I have been writing nothing else for years.

© Hastings-slush Productions

■ *Do you agree with Max about slush? Have you got a slush story? We'd love to hear it – or anything else to fill up our pages because most of our staff can't get in because of the slush.*

THE SNOWED-UNDER SOCIALISTS SINKING IN THE SLUDGE!   Fountain and Jamieson

INSIDE NUMBER TEN, THE NOO...

AH RECKON BY MA CALCULATIONS, IT'LL BE SIX MONTHS BEFORE THEY MANAGE TAE DIG US OOT...

BUT PA BROON, WE'RE NOT SNOWED IN! TH' SNOW'S ALL MELTED AWA LAST WEEK, YE KEN!

WHO SAID ANYTHING ABOOT SNOW?

HENRY DAVIES

WAR CRIMINAL TOO ILL TO FACE TRIAL

by Our War Crimes Staff **Lunchtime O'Bower**

A LONDON inquiry was yesterday the scene of a macabre spectacle when an accused war criminal was wheeled in on a trolley, claiming that he was too ill to speak.

"Hey, guys," he addressed the courtroom from his recumbent position, "I'd love to help out with your inquiry into the Iraq War, but I have suddenly been overcome by such a severe illness that I am physically incapable of testifying."

The tribunal chairman, Lord Didcot of Parkway, expressed his deepest sympathy with the accused, his old friend Tony Blair.

"The question to which this court demands an answer, Mr Blair, is whether you would like to go home to recover from this ordeal.

"I am sure," he went on severely, "that we could arrange an ambulance for you, to take you to lunch.

"Which reminds me," the learned chairman concluded, "I see that it is 12 o'clock and time for an adjournment for us all to go off to the Reform Club for luncheon."

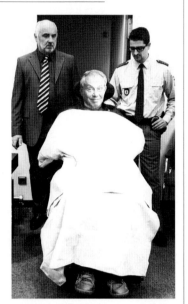

"…And yet you claimed you had irrefutable proof that the sky **was** falling down"

POLICE FAIL TO RESPOND TO STRAW ATTACK

by Our Crime Staff **John Desk-Sergeant**

JUSTICE SECRETARY Jack Straw yesterday sensationally accused the police of being "lazy". Yet 24 hours later no one from the police had responded to the charge.

Inspector Knackered

Said Mr Straw, "No officer has contacted me, no one has come round to see me and no one has even offered me counselling".

When this newspaper tried to contact the police for a statement, nobody answered the phone and a message informed us that "Scotland Yard is unable to take your call at present due to the fact that we can't be arsed".

"To be perfectly honest, Mrs Phillips, it's none of your business"

Mobile Phone Slightly Different From Other Mobile Phone Goes On Sale

by Our Technology Correspondent **Mike Twitter**

THE tech world was in uproar last night as it was rumoured that a mobile phone which was slightly different from mobile phones that are currently on sale would soon go on sale.

"It's almost impossible to comprehend how important it is that a mobile phone which is slightly different from mobile phones that are already on sale will soon go on sale," said one over-excited fat man in a tight-fitting black t-shirt, jumping up and down excitedly.

UNDERWEAR BOMBER SHOCK

I did nothing wrong

Liar! Liar! Pants on fire!

SIR JOHN CHILCOT

Do you start with any specific views on spoons?

Can I make it clear at the outset that I don't see it as my role to single out any particular spoon as superior or inferior to any other?

So how do you see your role on the spoon issue?

I am not in the business of praise or blame. I am here to give everyone the opportunity to talk about spoons in the frankest possible way – although of course there will be occasions when it is necessary for those views to be heard in secret.

Doesn't it look to the public as though you're engaged in some kind of a whitewash?

No. That would be absurd. You can't whitewash a spoon. Washing-up liquid, possibly, although I am quite open to alternatives, such as Spoon-o-Glit or Mr Gleem.

Has anything amusing ever happened to you in connection with a spoon?

██████████████████

(Sir John's answer to this question had to be given in secret)

NEXT WEEK: *Ron Wood – Me And My Wood.*

'I WOULD HAVE INVADED IRAQ EVEN IF BUSH HADN'T TOLD ME TO'

Blair's shock admission

by Our Religious Staff BILL GODDIE

ON THE first day of the wide-ranging BBC inquiry into the role of former prime minister Blair in the Iraq war, the chairman Sir Fernwell Britton asked the chief witness Mr Blair whether religion had played a big part in his life at 10 Downing Street.

"Look," said Britain's former war leader, "going into Iraq would have been the right thing to do, even if it was the wrong thing."

■ Watch again the full version of Fern Britton's incredible and history-making interview with the Rt. Hon. Tony Blair, which the BBC carefully broadcast early on Sunday morning at a time when nobody is watching (the so-called 'Frost slot') because it was about religion.

The Secret DIARY OF SIR JOHN MAJOR KG aged 87¾

I am not inconsiderably incandescent with rage, as I told my wife Norman this morning over our breakfast cereal of Golden Grahams. "I would not have invaded Iraq," I said. "Oh, no! Unlike Mr Blair, I always told the truth."

"Except about Mrs Curry," she replied, accidentally pouring a cup of hot tea over my head. "This is my WMD, which stands for Weapon of Major Destruction," she added, which was in no way necessary or amusing in my judgement.

What you will hear

Chilcot Enquiry Day 94
Evidence of Mr Alastair Campbell

Sir John Chilcot (*for it is he*): Thank you very much for coming in Mr Campbell, I know you are a very busy man.

Alastair Campbell: Don't patronise me you fucking Whitehall wanker. I know all about you and I know where you live and the same goes for the rest of you scumbags sitting there on your fat arses you can all fuck off.

Sir John Chilcot: Thank you very much indeed Mr Campbell, I think that covers everything.

"He's so gifted, don't you think?"

...WHO Y' LOOKIN' AT FOOL, GONNA BUST A CAP, BLOW Y' HEAD CLEAN OFF...

Neasden Central Police Station

1033 hrs Emergency call received from member of public to report suspicious person taking photographs of the sign above the hairdressing salon in Pricerite Road – The Cut Above. An armed response team was immediately dispatched to the scene of the crime, led by Det. Sgt. Moorgate. On arrival the suspect was identified as a Mr Barry Whittam-Smith, a retired gentleman who claimed that he had found the sign "amusing". When warned that he was committing an offence under Section 48 of the Prevention of Terrorism Act 2007, governing the making of photographic images of any building or other installation in public, Mr Whittam-Smith began to act in a highly suspicious manner by uttering the words "You must be joking". He then refused to give a blood sample or to give details of his ethnicity. He was tasered using the minimum strength of 50,000 volts and, due to an underlying medical condition, regrettably passed away before charges could be brought against him. No further action therefore needed to be taken.

1215 hrs Calls received from 59 members of the public reporting concern among residents of the Nelson Mandela housing estate, over a dangerous canine of unclassified breed being kept in proximity to under-age infants. No officers were available to investigate, owing to their attendance on a three-day training course on "Improving Relationships With The Muslim Community".

NEWS IN BRIEF

Britain 'Plunged Into Recovery'

Britain was reeling last night as the Office of National Statistics confirmed that the country had been plunged into recovery.

"The boom times of recession we've all enjoyed over the past 12 months are now coming to an end," warned one senior economist.

"And instead we have to look forward to the grim prospect of a long and painful recovery."

The Chancellor, however, insisted that the 0.1 per cent growth figure was just a statistical blip and that thanks to Labour's policies Britain would soon climb out of recovery and back into a prolonged recession again.

Public 'Won't Receive A Bonus'

The Chief Executive of the RBS, Stephen Hester, has confirmed that the public will be involuntarily waiving its share of the £1.3 billion in bonuses being paid out this year by the bank.

"The involuntary restraint shown by the public by receiving nothing from the bonus pool is admirable in these hard times," said the delighted Chief Executive.

Looking forward, Mr Hester said he was confident that the public would also receive no bonus next year, nor the year after that nor, with any luck, the year after that.

'WE WERE BETRAYED,' Claim Plotters

by Our Political Staff
Coup Stark-Raving-Mad

THE LABOUR Party was bitterly divided last night over what was described as a gross act of treachery by factions inside the Cabinet.

Said chief plotters Geoff Hoohee and Patricia Hewshe, "We were trying to betray Gordon and then we were betrayed by the Cabinet."

Lost The Curry House Plot

Hoohee and Hewshe continued, "We were stabbed in the back by all those cowards who promised us they would stab Gordon in the back."

"We wanted to replace a dithering indecisive leader. But everyone bottled out of it."

NIGHT OF THE LONG KNIVES

Et tu, Dave?

LATE NEWS: COUP FAILS

That Curry House Plot Menu In Full

Argy Bhaji
Mutter Paneec

– ✳ –

Chicken-Out Korma
Lame Vindaloser

– ✳ –

Served with
Chapatihewitt and
Vegetable Hoona

– ✳ –

To drink:
Bottled small beer

DR KELLY – HUTTON IN SHOCK U-TURN

LORD HUTTON, chairman of one of the many controversial Iraq inquiries, yesterday reversed his decision not to let the 13 doctors who think Dr Kelly was murdered see the secret papers that prove that they were right *(surely "that might cause undue distress to his family?" Ed.)*.

LATE NEWS

THIRTEEN doctors were last night found dead in a field. A police spokesman, Mr A. Campbell, said that all of the doctors had killed themselves by taking a huge overdose of two paracetamol tablets. One of them had also deliberately cut himself shaving.

"Excuse me. They won't let you take anything inflammatory onto the plane"

University of South East London & Essex
USELESS
Tomorrow's Knowledge Today

A Letter from the Vice-Chancellor
Sir Terry Spreadsheet Hon D. Litt, ASDA

It has been for me a busy first three months in my very challenging new role as Vice Chancellor of the thriving educational hub that is USELESS.

Already we can see the changes that I initiated being rolled out across every aspect of the University's functioning.

For instance, we have commissioned a feasibility study from management consultants KRAP to look into a possible merger of USELESS with six other institutes of higher education, to create Britain's first "Super University" with over half a million students.

This will allow us to compete on a level playing field with such giants of academia as the new University of Mid-Wales, Solihull and East Anglia.

Our £100 million building programme is going ahead on target, based on our new Tesco Centre for Retail Technology.

Styled "Work 'n' Learn" , this will be the first degree course offered by any university in the world where, for only £5,700 a term, students can develop their retailing skills in such modules as Shelf Product Allocation, Checkout Operation and Customer Feedback, with on-site mentoring from "real" managers.

We are all very excited at the response this new course is generating in many countries and take- up has been particularly high from Latvia, Kosovo and Zimbabwe.

Some of you may have read wildly inaccurate reports in the Times Higher Educational Supplement concerning the three-week fact-finding cruise made by my wife and myself around the Caribbean, supported by a 100 percent grant from the University's Longterm Academic Research Fund (LARF).

The newspaper's attempt to suggest that this was anything other than an entirely bona fide research project linked to our degrees in Tourism Studies, Marine Biology, Nautical Architecture and Climate Change, was a disgraceful example of the type of "gutter journalism" for which the THES has long been synonymous.

In order to protect the University's good name, the Governing Council have agreed to my suggestion that the University should retain the services of Messrs Carter Ruck, Shilling and Mishcon de Reya to demand a full retraction, apology and damages for these entirely baseless slurs on the reputation of the University.

On a happier note, I would like to record our pleasure that the University was able to confer an honorary degree on Mr Shifti Bakhanda, the Chairman of the Maldivian Tourist Authority.

May I finally close by commending the work of our USELESS Student Islamicist Jihadi Society, whose recent seminars ("Fighting The Great Satan") have been so successful, attracting attendees from as far afield as Yemen, Waziristan, Nigeria and Dewsbury.

These seminars did much to promote a greater understanding of the aims and purposes of Islamic fundamentalism.

It was only regrettable that one member of the Society was later involved in an unfortunate attempt to destroy much of London with a nuclear device.

There will always be a few rotten apples and people who get carried away, and this particular incident in no way undermines the important work we do here at USELESS.

Happy New Year
Sir Terry

Sir Terry Spreadsheet

Lookalikes

Miliband **Chimp**

Sir,

Has anyone else noticed the resemblance between renowned banana lovers, Labour leader hopeful, David Miliband, and the Musical Jolly Chimp? Might they perhaps be distantly related?

Yours sincerely,
DAVID FINLAY,
Via email.

Witch **Liz Jones**

Sir,

I wonder if your readers have noticed the similarity between the Wicked Witch of the West in The Wizard Of Oz and the Wicked Witch of the West Country in the Mail On Sunday.

Yours sincerely,
A. BENTLEY,

Louth.

Redknapp **Palmerston**

Sir,

If you don't use this, I'm cancelling my subscription etc. Lord Palmerston and Harry Redknapp share a striking resemblance and (judging from some of Harry's past signings) an adventurous approach to foreign policy.

Yours,
RORY TAYLOR,
Via email.

Burnham **Tracy**

Sir,

I recall Andy Burnham piloting Thunderbird 1 in the 1970's and thought he may be related to the MP for Leigh, Scott Tracy?

Yours,
DAN BOWDEN,
Via email.

Young Benny **Young Adrian**

Sir,

I am the only person to have noticed the startling resemblance between Adrian Chiles and the late Benny Hill?

Yours,
RUTH GRIMSLEY,
Sheffield.

Piers Morgan **Karen Gillard**

Sir,

Has anyone noticed the uncanny similarity between TV interviewer Piers "Morgan" Moron and the Liberal Democrats' prospective parliamentary candidate for South East Cornwall, Karen Gillard? While Ms Gillard was previously a Tory councillor, proving that a leopard can change its spots, Moron of course will always be a ****.

ENA B. KING,
London W8.

Gabor **Evans**

Sir,

Have any of your readers noticed, as I have, the astonishing resemblance between Zsa-Zsa Gabor, pictured recently in the press at the age of 92, and the DJ and broadcaster Chris Evans, who has recently taken over from Sir Terence Wogan, 92. I wonder if by any chance they are related?

Yours,
ENA B. PIPER,
Via email.

Lampard **Kafka**

Sir,

I couldn't help noticing that the well-known Chelsea midfielder Frank Kafka looks uncannily like he has metamorphosed from the iconic writer Franz Lampard.

Yours,
LANCE FENNELL,
Via email.

Lady Macbeth **Cherie Blair**

Sir,

In Stratford upon Avon, whilst admiring a group of statues depicting Shakespeare and some of his main characters, I could not help but notice the uncanny resemblance between Lady Macbeth and that other over ambitious wife of a tarnished leader, Mrs Cherie Blair. Is it possible that the two ladies are related?

Yours,
DAVID WESLEY,
Via email.

Iggle Piggle **PM**

Sir,

Tory critics of the ConLib coalition who complain that it concedes too much on policy should surely be reassured by the PM's ongoing commitment to true blue policies and the youth vote, finding time to appear under the pseudonym Iggle Piggle in In The Night Garden.

CHARLES WYNN-EVANS,
London, SE24.

Kirsty **Monica**

Sir,

I always wondered (not really) what happened to Monica Lewinsky... now I realise she's been on our TV screens for years, bossing that bald chap around, and telling people what houses they should buy, calling them all sorts when they don't like her suggestions.

She's really mastered the posh accent too...

SHARON DUNCAN,
Edinburgh.

Smeagol **Marr**

Sir,

Lord of the dead ringers?
JON WRIGHT,
London.

Moore   **Griffin**

Sir,

Could Americans be confusing their favourite "giant socialist weasel" for Family Guys Peter Griffin?

Regards,
ANDREW KEEN,

Buxton.

Shroud   **Forsyth**

Sir,

I couldn't help noticing the resemblance between that gruesome medieval fake Bruce Forsyth and the all-singin', all-dancin' entertainer the Turin Shroud. Should Brucie's jokes be carbon-dated?

Best wishes,
RICHARD WOODWARD,

Via email.

Crypt Keeper   **Prince of Darkness**

Sir,

Have others noticed the similarities between these creepy long-running serialisations – Tales from the Crypt and the Mandelson Memoir? I shudder to think of the Prince of Darkness' next instalment.

Yours,
TOM HOYLE,

Via email.

Foreign Minister   **Scarecrow**

Sir,

I see we have the Scarecrow from the Wizard of Oz as the new EU Foreign Minister (Lady Ashton). He of course had no brain, but who then is the Cowardly Lion, or the Tin Man with no heart or indeed Dorothy?

G.M. FRASER,

Via email.

Blair   **Donovan**

Sir,

Re Jason Donovan and Tony Blair.
I wonder if any of your readers have noticed the similarity between the unconvincing former soap opera actor and Mr Jason Donovan...?

Yours ever,
DAN HARRISON,

Via email.

Fabio   **Mel B**

Sir,

I fear I may have discovered the cause of the England team's performance in this year's World Cup. Clearly they are being coached by one of Avid Merrion's rubber-faced creations from the Channel 4 show "Bo Selecta".

Yours,
ZAK QUINEY,

Via email.

Dummy   **Gove**

Sir,

I wonder if any of your older readers have noticed the striking resemblance between Tory Education Secretary Michael Gove and ventriloquist's dummy Archie Andrews, popular on radio in the 1950s?

Yours sincerely,
DAVE TAYLOR,

Purbrook, Hampshire.

Midwitch Cuckoo   **Martin Amis**

Sir,

Many may have wondered how an intelligent man like Martin Amis can hold such misanthropic views about old people and their place in society. May I venture a suggestion?

CHARLIE TURNER,

Via email.

Lourdes Virgin   **Swinton**

Sir,

I recently visited the Basilica of the Rosary at Lourdes. I wonder whether any of your readership has been struck, as was I, by the extraordinary likeness between its mosaic of the Virgin Mary and the actress Tilda Swinton?

Yours etc,
ROBERT STIRLING,

Via email.

Vespasian   **Crow**

Sir,

After his triumphant appearance on Have I Got News For You, I was delighted to see that a grateful travelling public has erected a monument to the saviour of the British railway, Bob Crow.

Yours,
MARK DORRINGTON,

Cobham, Surrey.

Gummidge   **Hammond**

Sir,

I can't help but notice the striking similarity between Richard Hammond and Wurzel Gummidge.

Are the two the same, and the result of an excellent re-branding exercise on the part of Mr Gummidge's agent?

Regards,
NIGEL BALDWIN,

Maidenhead.

Alien   **Balls**

Sir,

Has anyone else noticed the uncanny resemblance between the civic-minded progressive Labour leadership candidate Ed Balls and the vicious killer alien from the movie "The Predator"?

WILLIAM SHAW,

Via email.

RICH PEOPLE HAVE MORE MONEY THAN POOR PEOPLE – NEW REPORT

by Our Social Affairs Correspondent **Ann Thropology**

A SHOCK new report, compiled by the Government-funded think-tank ISBO (Institute for Stating the Bleeding Obvious), has come up with a startling conclusion that in the Britain of 2010 rich people are still better off than poor people.

The report's key findings will make unhappy reading for government ministers, recalling Tony Blair's promise in 1997 that he was going to eliminate poverty.*

Rich people, the researchers found, tended to have:

- more money
- bigger houses
- wider TV screens
- more expensive cars
- top-of-the-range barbecue sets (not B&Q, Homebase, Asda etc)
- luxury trouser presses in every room.

Said the leader of the study, Professor Ron Damp of Nottingham Metropolitan University, "It is depressing that in this day and age rich people are still richer than poor people. It makes me ashamed to be Canadian."

* Read the report in full online at www.dullanddreary.org.

A Taxi Driver writes

EVERY week a well-known cab driver is invited to comment on an issue of topical importance.

This week **Marty Amis** (Cab No. 1732) on Britain's ageing population explosion .

Bloody old people, look at them, guv. They're every-where, queueing up with their bus passes, trying to cross the road, oi, get out the way grandad! I could've killed 'im, guv. Come to think of it, it's not a bad idea. I mean, let's be honest, we can't have the country swamped by millions and millions of stinking old gits. Tell you my idea, guv. No, we don't string 'em all up, I'm not a nutter. What we do is have all these little booths, like those toilets they have on the Continent, and all the old people can go in and put themselves to sleep. What's wrong with that? By the way, I've got another new book out. Do you want a signed copy – I've got loads in the boot, can't get rid of them! Unlike the old people, eh? Ha, ha, ha!

NEXT WEEK: Anatole Kaletsky on "Why I've been warning of a double-dip recession for years".

An Apology

IN RECENT months we may have given the impression that Barack Obama was a political colossus, a superman who bestrode the American political stage like no leader had before him, who had rewritten the rule book in Washington. An inspirational leader whose soaring oratory had united the American people behind his powerful slogan of change – "Yes, we can!".

We now realise in the light of the Republican, Scott Brown, winning the Senate race in Massachusetts that nothing could be further from the truth, and that Barack Obama is in fact a hopelessly naïve dreamer who clearly doesn't understand that you have to play by the Washington rule book. His inept leadership and empty rhetoric has united the American people in rejecting his trite and embarrassing slogan of change – "Yes, we can!".

We apologise for any confusion caused and any confusion in the future when Obama manages to get his health reform bill passed against the odds and we hail him as a political colossus, etc, etc, etc.

"Wow! We've never wasted time as fast as this before"

B&B COUPLE IN ADMISSION REFUSAL ROW

by Our Political Staff **Gay Right**

A DEVOUT Christian couple who run a small bed and breakfast have defended their decision to refuse to allow Tories to stay overnight on their premises.

Said the couple, "According to our beliefs, being a Conservative is not natural and the things they get up to are, frankly, immoral."

Chris Gayling

When asked to elaborate, the couple said, "They could be doing anything in that room. Fiddling with each other's expenses, claiming that our B&B was their second home, or performing unpleasant acts of what we gather consenting Tories call 'Lobbying'."

A Conservative spokesman said, "The views of this couple are completely outdated. Everyone accepts that there is no longer a stigma attached to being a practising Conservative".

He concluded, "We are much more tolerant nowadays as a community, which is why we should bring back hanging and string these bigots up".

WHO WERE THEY – THE FACES THAT DEFINED THE NOUGHTIES?

by Radio 4's Voice of the Decade **Jim Noughtie**

IT WAS the best of decades, it was the worst of decades. When it began, we had no idea how it would end.

When it ended, we had no idea how it had begun.

They called it "the dangerous decade", "the decadent decade", even "the naughty Noughties".

It was the decade of 9/11, 10/11, 7/7, 24/7 and 11/9.

It was the decade which gave us new words: Tsunami, Credit Crunch, Berlusconi and Trouser Press.

It was the decade which began with Bush and ended with Obama.

But throughout those ten years a succession of new talents exploded into our consciousness, helping to define who we were and where we were going.

Here are six of those meteors who flashed across the Noughties sky *(Get on with it. Ed.)*:

Fratelli Cornetto, 46, Italian-born handbag designer whose luminous "clutch bags" were the must-have fashion accessory of the decade.

Kevin McNugget, 31, Glasgow-born celebrity chef who took the world of cuisine by storm through his hit TV show, *Fuckit It's McNugget*.

Emmy Wino, 25, troubled female vocalist whose debut album, *Pissed Again*, sold more copies than any in music history. Thanks to her personal demons, fans are still eagerly awaiting the 2010 relaunch album *Still Pissed*.

Jimmy Gotz and **Dave Goldberg**, the 31-year-old geniuses behind the social networking site My Face which, within three weeks of its launch from their uncle's North London garage, had 30 million subscribers, including Tony Blair and Stephen Fry.

T.B. Gidman, 52, the children's fantasy author whose seven-part trilogy *The Curse of the Mandelson* netted the former schoolmaster £23 billion by the end of the decade. Now a series of films starring Stephen Fry as the dark sorcerer Mandy.

Chris Halfords, 28, the Wigan-born super-cyclist whose haul of 29 gold medals in the Ankara Winter Olympics set a record never likely to be broken. No one will forget his legendary triumph over the Swiss world champion Klaus Santer in the 25 kilometre road pursuit time trial at the Kemal Ataturk Velodrome. *(That's enough Noughties. Ed.)*

GLENDA SLAGG
She likes 'em young!!

■ HERE'S to you Mrs Robinson!!?! *(They've all done this one. You're fired. Ed.)* Hats and knickers off to you Mrs Robinson!!?! *(That's better. Ed.)* You've taken a pickaxe single-handedly to centuries-old stuck-up Northern Irish prudery and sent it crashing to the floor!!?! Tell me, Rev O'Killjoy with your daft bowler hat and your orange sash – what's so wrong about a dishy dame a-kissin' and a-kuddlin' with a kute little kiddie young enough to be her grandson!?!! Here's to you Mrs Robinson – I say it again!?!! *(You're fired again. Ed.)*

■ IRIS ROBINSON – what a disgrace!??!! Here's a randy old granny from the land of peat 'n' potato a-gawpin' and a-gropin' with some helpless mite scarcely out of short trousers!!?! With your raunchy love romps you've single-handedly dragged Northern Ireland back to the Middle Ages!!?! Peace Process? Peace-Off Process is my preferred solution!!?! Geddit?!

■ SUSAN TOLLEFSEN – she's the would-be 59-year-old mum-to-be who wants a test-tube toddler to comfort her twilight years!?!! And why not, mister?!?? Isn't it every pensioner's right to have an interest to keep her going through the day!!?! And what better than a lovely little nipper a-burblin' and a-burpin' as life's nights draw in!!?! IVF – I Vote Foryou, Susan!? Geddit?!?

■ SUSAN TOLLEFSEN – have you gone stark staring bonkers?!?? When most women of your age are getting their bus pass and baking cakes for the WI, you're cooking up a bun in the oven!?!! Who do you think you are?!?? Iris Robinson?!??!?

■ HERE THEY ARE – Glenda's Twenty-Ten Toy Boys!?!

● **Chris Evans!?!!** Wake up with Ginger – I can think of worse fates!?!!?

● **Chris Ofili**. The art world's Mr Elephant Dung!?!! They tell me you're Ofili good in bed!?!! Geddit?!?

● **Mutasim-Billah Gaddafi!?!** Crazy name, crazy guy!?!!

Byeee!!

'STUPID PEOPLE SHOULDN'T BE ALLOWED TO GIVE INTERVIEWS' claims Ricky Gervais

by Our Showbiz Staff **Stephen Merchandise**

IN ONE of only 94 interviews in this week's newspapers, reluctant celebrity and TV funnyman Ricky Gervais caused national outrage when he attacked the right of stupid people to reproduce their ill-thought-out views in interviews.

"If you see a fat bloke with a beard and a big mouth, then he shouldn't be allowed to give interviews. Fact," he told the *Sunday Times*.

A spokesman for Mr Gervais later claimed that "Ricky was only joking". He said, "If you don't think that is funny then Ricky will move to New York where they appreciate genius and don't try to criticise celebrities like Ricky who are only trying to do their job criticising other celebrities. Fact."

"Dammit Frankenstein, you're wasting our time"

THAT BLAIR CHILCOT APPEARANCE IN FULL

hour 94

Lord Didcot of Parkway: And carrying on from Baroness Rubesh's last question may I return to the meeting with President Bush in 2002? (*fumbles with notes*). What exactly was agreed concerning an acceptable *casus belli* for an invasion of Iraq?

Rev Blair: Hey, I'm really glad you asked that, but what's really important to remember is that the situation in 2002 was very different then to what it is now. And looking at it in perspective the issues that seem important now that you are asking questions about, quite justifiably, weren't necessarily those that were important then, so you see (*reads out soundbite from notes*) it wasn't a deception, it was a decision (© A. Campbell).

Sir Gilbert Martin: (*waking up*) Where am I? I can't seem to find my bedroom slippers.

Rev Blair: Hey, isn't that the whole point. The fact that you can't find something doesn't mean it's not there. Look at WMDs. Imagine what would have happened if they *had* been there? That's the question we should be asking isn't it?

Sir Lawrence Freeride: So what would have happened, Mr Blair, if you had found the WMDs?

Rev Blair: Well to begin with you wouldn't be asking these questions, Sir Lawrence. If we hadn't acted as we did, Saddam would now probably be engaged in a nuclear war with Iran, which might easily escalate and conceivably destroy the whole world within the next 45 minutes. I mean, who would want that? You see, that's what I had to consider then, I was in charge, I had to take responsibility for getting rid of a monster and saving millions of innocent lives. People are free to blame me for that and I respect that because we live in a democracy, unlike Saddam by the way, but hey (*reads out soundbite from notes*) it wasn't lying, it was leading (© A. Campbell).

Baroness Uttar Rubbesh: Could I ask you what assurances you made to Fern Britton at your historic meeting with her in December 2009?

Rev Blair: Look, we had a meeting. We discussed a number of issues, that's what you do when you're in the top job. But hey, no-one was making notes and Fern was doing a remarkable job and I sat knee to knee with her and told her that whatever happened I was there for her and I can say all this now because now is now and that was then and whatever might have happened didn't. So the answer to your question, which is a very good one, is exactly what you might expect. It was my job to answer – mine alone – and look (*reads soundbite from notes*) this isn't about evasion, it's about invasion (© Alastair Campbell).

Rubbesh: Thank you very much.

Sir Lawrence FreeIraq: May I now ask you, Mr Blair, about the speech you made in Chicago in 1999 when you put the case for intervention and by extension regime change in failed states?

Rev Blair: Of course you can ask about the speech, Sir Lawrence. You wrote it.

Sir Friedman: Oh yes, so I did. Shall we go to lunch?

Rev Blair: I think that's a very good question. Because let's face it, we have a choice. Either we decide to go to lunch or we decide not to go. Whatever we decide there are going to be people who disagree. That's the territory, that's the nature of the job (*reads soundbite from notes*). It's not about legality, it's about Brown Windsor soup…hang on, that can't be right.

Sir Martin Dormouse: Did someone mention Brown Windsor soup?

Lord Didcot of Parkway: I think now would be a good time for us to adjourn.

Do you have any regrets?

I should have invaded Iran as well

Thank you for coming

Ah WELL, IT'S ALL PART of...

DON'T SAY IT!

INDEPENDENT REPORT SLAMS BBC SPENDING

by Our Media Staff **Jane Thynnke-Tank**

THE BBC is wasting millions of pounds of licence-payers' money, claimed a controversial new report yesterday, and it singled out hugely expensive programmes like *Met Men*.

Said the report, "Enormous sums of money are ploughed into *Met Men*, but the result has been very disappointing. Most viewers have complained that *Met Men* looks good, but actually gets everything wrong."

The report continued with its harsh criticism of the programme, concluding: "*Met Men* is entirely unbelievable. The episodes *Barbecue Summer* and *Mild Winter*, in particular, were notable for their levels of inaccuracy and smugness."

A spokesman for *Met Men*, however, defended the multi-billion-pound weather show and said, "One thing is for sure. No one is going to say that *Met Men* is a waste of money and the BBC shouldn't be funding it."

Guardian Supremo To Run easyJet

by Our Business Staff **Phil Pockets**

Carolyn McCall, the former chief executive of the Guardian Media Group, is to take over the budget airline easyJet.

Passengers can look forward to a radical shake-up of the business and will soon see the following changes:

- Smaller "Berliner" size aircraft
- The closing down of the Sunday Flight Operation
- Huge expansion of the easyJet website where you can get flights for free instead of paying for them at travel agent
- Celebrity wallpaper to be given away to regular flyers
- easyJet to be misprinted as esayJet (or possibly aseyJeta) (*That's enough, Ed*).

HAITI
The Post Mortem

by Our Men In Port-au-Prince **Phil Plane** and **Phil Airport**

"This is Katie Jones reporting exclusively..."

AS WE look back on the tragedy which has shocked the world, one question above all others demands an answer.

Why did it take so long for the world's media to get through to the victims of this disaster?

In the immediate aftermath of the earthquake, the world watched in horror as hundreds of reporters were reduced to interviewing each other, instead of supplying the world with "very disturbing images" of dead people.

How, the world is asking, could there have been such a lack of infrastructure and organisation that many of the most committed and respected journalists in the world could not drive along proper roads to a five-star hotel, but were forced to wait around in the airport asking the cleaners whether they knew what was going on?

Said one leading journalist whom we interviewed shortly after he had interviewed us, "No wonder we have all decided to go home after a couple of days. I mean, there's no hope of rescuing a story from under all that rubble. I'm off."

● Full story, distressing pictures, and badly-timed advertisement for "Two Weeks In Haiti Cruise Offer" – pages 2-94.

THOSE HAITIAN DISASTERS

Papa Doc

Baby Doc

No Docs

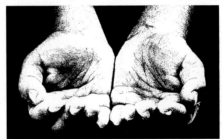
The Alternative Rocky Horror Service Book

No. 94 A Service Of Confirmation Of A Place For The Child Of An Atheist At A CofE School.

The President (for it is he or she): Brethren and sistren, we are gathered here today to welcome into our congregation Mr and Mrs M_ or M_ (he may say here "Miliband") who wish their child to attend our CofE primary school because it is much better than the local State school next to where they live.

Congregation: Indeed it is.

President: Shall we start with the Creed?

Congregation: I don't believe in God the Father Almighty or all the rest of that stuff, but I do believe in my right to send my child to a church school that scores high in the league tables. Amen.

Reading from The Letter To The Guardian, Ch. 13, v. 13

Reader: Dear Sir, there is nothing hypocritical in a parent trying to do the best for their children, even if that parent happens to be a practising atheist and a senior minister in a government that strongly disapproves of selective faith schools. Of course it is right that these schools should be abolished immediately. But since they still exist, it is quite right for us to take advantage of the fact that they are much better than our incomparably excellent State schools... er... Yours faithfully, Dame Polly Spart, Chair of Hackney Council Education Committee.

All: Thanks be to Gordon.

President: We shall now sing Hymn 94, "O Happy Miliband Of Pilgrims (if onward ye will tread)".

YES! IT'S WORLD ⚽ CUP WILLY! ⚽

They think it's all legover...

...it is now!

GLENDA SLAGG
The WAG They Can't Gag!?!!?

■ **HATS OFF** to Two-Timing **Terry!?!!** England's sex-crazed skipper who can't keep his shorts up!?!! OK, so Terry bonked his team mate's missus and knocked her up whilst he was away!?!! He's a footballer, for Gawd's sake, Mr Killjoy, he's not the Archbishop of Canterbury!??!! It's what the beautiful game is all about?!? Beautiful blokes and busty birds a-jumpin' and a-humpin' all over the place!?! Good on you, John!!?! Who cares about the miserable missus and krying kiddies!?!!

■ **JOHN TERRY** – what a disgrace!??!! You should pull up your shorts and hang your head in shame!?! What kind of role model are you, Jiltin' John?!?? A roll-in-the-sack model more like!?!! Geddit? And talking of the sack – that's what Fabio should give you!?!! And what about the mistreated missus and the tearful toddlers?!? What thought have you given them?!?? Eh?!? Dad of the Year?!? *Cad* of the Year, more like!?!! Geddit?!?

■ *TIGER WOODS!?!* Now he says he's suffering from sex addiction!!?! Who does he think he is?!? John Terry?!??!

■ SEE Manchester United in 3D on the telly?!?! I'd rather be watching John Terry playing away!?!?!

■ HERE THEY ARE – Glenda's Valentine's Day Valentinos?!?!

● **Keith Schilling!?!!** Mr Super-injunction, they call him!!?! You can come round and gag me with your big writ anytime!?!!

● **Mr Justice Tugendhat**. Hats off to Britain's Sexiest Judge!?!! Fancy invading my privacy, Your Lordship – cos I'm gagging for it!?! Geddit?!?

● **President Jacob Zuma!?!** Crazy name, crazy wives!?!!

Byeee!!

TERRY'S GIRLFRIEND

Of course I took precautions ...I phoned Max Clifford

THE ⚜ TIMES
Friday, February 5 1855

Light Brigade Inquiry

LORD CARDIGAN
'It Was A Terrific Success'
by Our Military Staff **W.M. Deedes**

Lord Cardigan made a spirited defence of his controversial decision to charge into the Valley of Death, which resulted in hundreds of British casualties.

"We had reliable intelligence that the Russian guns were where we thought. The fact that they weren't makes no difference to my decision to charge."

He continued, "It wasn't a blunder, as some irresponsible people including the Poet Laureate seem to think. It was the right thing to do and I would do it again to bring about an end to the Light Brigade (Surely "Crimean War"? Ed.)."

■ *Full engraving and poem p. 94.*

■ *What do you think? Cardigan – right or wrong? Write us a letter and have your man deliver it to our club, The Army and Navy, Piccadilly.*

recent

A History of the World in 100 Objects, Radio 4.

TIM BALES

FOR CLEESE A JOLLY LUCKY FELLOW!!

YES, top funny-man John Cleese has found true romance at last with his new girlfriend, Anne Other-Blonde, 32.

Former Monty Python star and Fawlty Towers legend John looked relaxed and happy as he strolled hand in hand in the spring sunshine with lovely Anne.

Said one observer (of the photograph sent in to the picture desk), "Anne is clearly the one for much-married Ministry of

Silly Walks man, John.

"And one thing is certain, this time round she's definitely not going to clear off and take all John's money leaving him skint and depressed."

On other pages

■ *Cleese Interview:* "This relationship is over. It has ceased to be. It is an ex-relationship."

Great Scottish Clans No. 94

The McFuggers of McFugger

ONE OF the oldest and noblest of the Scottish clans, the McFuggers claim direct descent from the great Celtic Pharaoh Rameses II.

From ancient times, the McFuggers were feared and loathed as they went on the rampage, coming down from the Highlands selling carpets, grand pianos and luxury items of food.

Today the clan is headed by President Mohamed al-Fugger Of That Kilt, who wants Scotland to be independent under his leadership and who has waged a one-man war on the hated English Royal Family, and in particular the Duke of Edinburgh, who he describes as a "Fugging Sassenach murderer who should be run through with a fuggin' claymore."

With his famous battle-cry

of "Och aye the noo passport!", McFugger remains a fearsome figure as he stalks through Harrods looking for young women to *(Is this right? Ed)*.

"And this app allows you to conjure up the Devil"

GREEKS DEMAND RETURN OF 'HISTORIC TREASURE'

by Our Economic Staff **Lord Elgin**

THE GREEK Government today demanded the return of £26 billion worth of historic money from Britain.

"This money is ours" said the Greek Minister for Culture, Mr Enormaslos, "It shouldn't be in Britain it should be in Greece, the home of democracy and the birthplace of European Economic Crises *(Surely "culture"? Ed.)*

Spending Frieze

The British Government persist in claiming that the money technically belongs to Britain.

Said a spokesman, Mr Fred Needle, "It is much better for the money to be kept here where we know how to look after it – rather than giving it to the Greeks where it will end up ruins."

He concluded, "If the Greeks really think we're going to bail them out for their incompetence then they have clearly lost their marbles."

The Parthenon is 2,500 years old.

25 YEARS OF EASTENDERS

The Key Moments That Define The Age of Albert Square

1985

> Leave it out

1993

> Oi, shut it!

1998

> Not on my manor!

2004

> I don't believe I'm hearing this

2010

> Oi! Shut it! Leave it out! Not on my manor. I don't believe I'm hearing this

---

Lines on the Intervention by ex-Speaker Michael Martin, now Baron Martin of Springburn, in a House of Lords Debate on Libel Reform

BY **WILLIAM REES-McGONAGALL** *(Nominated By Sean Connery As Scottish Poet Of The Millennium)*

'Twas in the year Two Thousand and Ten,
When the disgraced Gorbals Mick took his seat in the House of Lords and then,
Instead of sitting there quietly, appreciating his good luck,
He jumped up to defend his greedy lawyers Messrs Carter *(cont. p.94)*

Court Circular

State visit of the South African premier, President Shagga Zulu

The procession will be formed as follows.

1st Carriage

Her Majesty Queen Brenda the First and President Shagga Zulu

2nd Carriage

His Royal Highness the Duke of Edinburgh;
Mrs Ludmilla Zuma

3rd Carriage

His Royal Highness the Prince of Wales; Mrs Mlegova Zuma; Mrs Rumpapumpa Zuma; Mrs Tutzi Frutzi Zuma; Mrs Bonkagogo Zuma

4th Carriage

Her Royal Highness The Duchess of Cornwall (2nd wife of HRH Prince Charles); Grand Witch Doctor and Keeper of the Magic Anti-Aids Shower, Dr Looni Mbarmi

1st stretch limousine

President Shagga's official ladies in waiting including 94 members of the Sin City Stripperama Experience

1st minibus

Master Keith Zuma, Miss Stacey Zuma, Master Wayne Zuma, Miss Jordan Zuma, Master Clint Zuma, Miss Subo Zuma and 82 others; Sir Alan Fitztightly, chief equerry to his Royal Highness

1st pram

Baby Buma Zuma
(That's enough carriages, Ed.)

GOD IS JOLLY GOOD!

THE NEW TESTAMENT
AS REPORTED BY FOX NEWS

"Hold it here! Healing isn't free! If he hasn't got healthcare insurance, then there's no healing!"

OPERATION 'COMPLETE SURPRISE' ABOUT TO START

by Our Military Staff **R.U. Ready**

THE Army has announced the launch of a major operation against the Taliban in Afghanistan which has been given the secret code name of Operation Complete Surprise.

General Sir Ivor Bigge-Mowthe told reporters, "Operation Complete Surprise will catch the Taliban totally off their guard."

Giving full details of exactly where and when all the military strikes will take place, the General told journalists, "This operation is foolproof and should be an historic success provided of course the enemy don't get wind of it beforehand."

Other observers, however, claimed that there was sound military commonsense behind the announcement of Operation Complete Surprise, as it would ensure that the enemy would run away and that there would be no civilian casualties.

Stop Press
- **Soldiers killed in firefight**
- **20 civilians dead in friendy fire incident**

WHO ARE THEY?

The Notting Hill Tories Whose Feuding Is Tearing The Party In Two

Joanna Tweetie, 40. *Chosen by Twitler Magazine as one of '10 Top Tory Toffettes to Watch'.* Young, glamorous modern high-flying barrister, married to millionaire hedge fund manager. Joanna has been parachuted into the safe London seat of Tottyham Court Road by her close friend David Cameron but has now resigned or possibly not according to her latest postings on Twitter: "Hi! What a day!?! DC is on message against the Dinosaurs!! Oh and by the way I'm preggers!? Ciaoo!!"

Mandy Twinsett, 50. Not so young, glamorous, high-flying barrister married to millionaire banker who has resigned as chairman of Tottyham Court Road Conservative Association, or has she? As she told friends: "I'm not having that Tweetie Bitch as candidate whatever Cameron thinks."

Octavius Pratt, 45. Old Etonian and founder of the Management Consultancy 'Mind the Gap' whose stated aim is to take a lot of money from large stupid corporations by talking a lot of bullshit. *(Is this right? Ed.)* A school friend of David Cameron, Octavius is very well connected in the party and at his wedding to Joanna the best man's speech was given by high-flying Shadow Cabinet star Hugh Onslow-Culpepper.

Eric Pickled-Onion, 78. Obese, non-Etonian, low-flying Party Chairman catapulted into his position by David Cameron to "bring a few oiks into the Party to show that we haven't all been to Eton". Pickled Onion's brief is to sort out the feud in Tottyham Court Road and to make sure it doesn't get into the newspapers and make the party look ridiculous.

JUST HANG ON WHILE I DEAL WITH THIS BASTARD

BRR! BRRR!

Cluff

Fashion genius shows the way

by Our Fashion Staff
Hilary Alexander McQueen

AFTER the shock death yesterday of the greatest fashion genius ever to have lived, fashionistas all over the world were rushing to hang themselves. *(Is this right? Ed.)*

Said one leading fashion editor, Anna Rexia, "Alexander McQueen was the most important and influential trendsetter in the entire history of this planet. Anyone who ever went to one of his shows came away literally shattered by the breathtaking display of creative and artistic brilliance combined with elements of satire, philosophy, history and S & M." *(Surely 'M&S'? Ed.)*

Bum Steers

And it is true. From see-through trousers to back-to-front shirts, from ankle-length mini-skirts to platform flip-flops the fertile mind of Alexander McQueen knew no boundaries.

And what McQueen did today the world will do tomorrow. And that means suicide. *(Are you sure about this? Ed.)*

Said King's Road icon, Tristram Loon, "We'll all be doing it now it's got the McQueen stamp of approval. Mark my words, we'll all be dead in a fortnight."

On other pages
- Is wearing black the new black?
- Is dead the new alive? *(You're fired. Ed.)*
- *Are you offended by the above piece? Why not cancel your subscription to Private Eye now. Simply ring the Eye's "End-It-All-Now" hotline and help send the magazine's record circulation figures plummeting.*

Assisted Cancellation Service
079422 56742817

ARCHBISHOP JOINS 'RIGHT TO DIE' DEBATE

BY OUR RELIGIOUS STAFF
RUTH GLEDTIDINGS

THE RIGHT Reverend Rowan Williams today weighed into the controversy over the "assisted suicide" debate which has caused a dangerous split in the ranks of the Church of England.

Addressing the general Synod, the Archbishop said, "However sympathetic we may feel, we cannot morally condone the killing off of the Church of England simply because we feel it is terminally ill and has no useful life ahead of it."

He continued, "It may be suffering from all kinds of splits and schisms tearing it apart, women bishops, flying bishops, gay bishops, African bishops who want to string up gay bishops, but that does not justify consciously putting an end to the church."

- **Sermon in full *p.94*.**

BANX

"I don't want anyone to think I might be gay"

Starting today – the most sensational
political biography ever written

'100 Things You Already Knew About Gordon Brown'

TOP Westminster insider Andrew Graunsley blows the lid off the simmering cauldron that is at the heart of power in Britain today.

In a series of shattering revelations, ace political analyst Graunsley discloses for the first time such astonishing facts as that:

● Gordon Brown has a very short temper and is often rude to people, according to top Whitehall sources

● Many of his colleagues, say trusted insiders, don't like him very much

● The Prime Minister once brushed past a senior civil servant in a Number Ten corridor and didn't even stop to say "sorry", according to first-hand witnesses of the incident who have spoken personally about it for the first time to author Graunsley

● World leaders are unanimous in their admiration for the shrewd and skilful way in which Brown rescued the global financial system (is this right? Ed).

Daily Mail

COMMENT

A Culture of Bullying?

YE GODS! What a lot of fuss about nothing! So some pathetic wimps in Number Ten have been whingeing about Gordon Brown's 'so-called' bullying!

For heaven's sake – surely we all know that the best bosses throughout the whole of history have always been those who were tough enough to get things done.

Think of Winston Churchill, Mrs Thatcher, Atilla the Hun, Adolf Hitler?! You don't think *they* achieved greatness by being shrinking violets and asking the PC Brigade for permission every time they wanted to lose their temper!

No! The only way for a great boss to express true leadership is to get his subordinates into his office and tell them that they are f***ing useless c***s who should be thrown out the f***ing window and never work for the f***ing Daily Mail ever again!!

© Paul Dacre, The Daily Mail 2010

GORDON BROWN'S SCHOOL DAYS

by Thomas Hughes-Heegh

"PLEASE STOP" cried the terrified schoolboy, as the evil bullies roasted his backside in front of the open fire. "I promise I'll never disagree with you again."

Tears rolled down his poor little face, as the smell of his singed flesh filled the Prefect's study.

But the callous cad who exercised a reign of terror over the younger boys was unmoved.

"Not so cocky now are you, Flashman, you snivelling little creep?" sneered Gordon Brown, as he gave the sobbing new boy a well aimed kick in the groin.

"That'll teach you to call me a bully!" he added.

Brown's cronies sniggered and the bloated features of Balls and McBride erupted into cruel grins.

"You'll get expelled for bullying, Gordon!" cried a desperate Flashman. "Just wait until I tell our saintly Headmaster, Mr Rawnsley, all about it."

But the wicked Brown laughed again and threw a recently invented fax machine at the hapless fag's head.

"I'm not a bully. I'm just passionate, strong-willed, determined..." said Gordon.

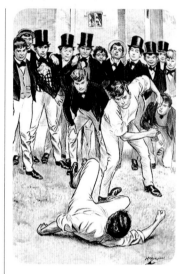

His toadying cohorts rapidly chimed in: "A strong leader... committed... Focused..."

"Doesn't suffer fools gladly," said Balls.

"A total bastard," added McBride unwisely, as Gordon Brown immediately lost his temper and flushed McBride's head down the school toilet.

THE bells of Westminster School chimed out as, at last, justice was done and the kind Flashman was sent home and Gordon Brown was made Head Boy again unopposed and went on to become the greatest Prefect the world had ever seen. *(Is this right? Ed.)*

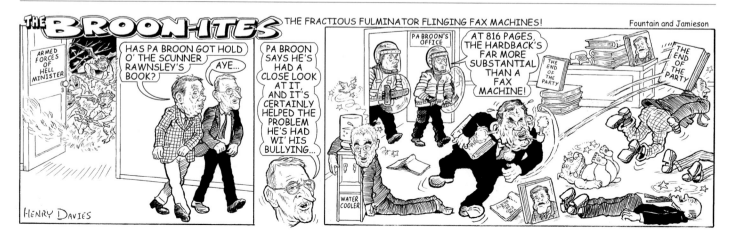

THE BROON-ITES

THE FRACTIOUS FULMINATOR FLINGING FAX MACHINES!

Fountain and Jamieson

HENRY DAVIES

DARLING ADMITS 'I RANG BULLYING HELPLINE'

by Our Bullying Staff **John Bully**

IN A sensational twist to Bully-gate, Chancellor Alistair Darling last night confessed that he was the one who rang up the National Bullying Helpline to complain about his treatment at the hands of Prime Minister Gordon Brown.

"It was the lowest moment of my life," said Mr Darling. "All I did was to say in an interview that the economy was looking a bit dodgy, and suddenly all hell broke loose.

"Gordon and his friends were really horrid to me throughout a whole weekend.

"They said nasty things about me in the media behind my back.

A scared Darling pictured in his office yesterday

The only word for it is bullying. "I was in such despair that I eventually rang the helpline."

"If you see this man, don't approach him. He's got lots of paperwork to do..."

PRIVATE EYE SOLD

LORD O'GNOME writes: I am delighted to announce that after fifty years of publishing I have decided that in order to guarantee the future of the magazine I must sell Private Eye to the highest bidder. (£1).

The purchaser is a highly respected Russian businessman, a Mr. Stalin, a former senior executive of the KGB and an obvious choice to take over a liberal British publication.

Mr. Stalin is no stranger to the UK Press having already rescued one national institution, the giveaway freesheet "What's on in Milton Keynes".

The huge success of Mr. Stalin and his son, Mr. Stalin Junior, in turning around the fortunes of this iconic giveaway bodes well for the future of Private Eye.

Mr Stalin told me: "I have long valued your British traditions" he said, "Free speech, free expression and free newspapers!"

And he explained his plans for Private Eye.

"Of course there will be changes. But I give my solemn pledge that none of those journalists currently working at Private Eye will be stabbed with umbrellas or poisoned by sushi meals for one"

Signed
Lord O'Gnome
Bally Wealthy,
County Money,
Ireland.

Your Guide To Those Coles, The Family Who are On The Front Page Of Every Newspaper In The Land

Cheryl Cole, 24-year-old beautiful, tragic, diminutive, sexy nation's sweetheart whose picture is always on the front page of newspapers.

Ashley Cole, 25-year-old good-looking, rich footballer, married to the above until yesterday. His picture used to be on the back page of every newspaper, but is now on the front page, as well as on the phones of various busty models.

John Cole, 86-year-old former Northern Irish political commentator, famous for his TV catchphrase "Hondootedly!" Father of Ashley (see above).

Nat King Cole, 106-year-old one-time international singing sensation, often pictured on the front of album covers singing "Mona Lisa". Uncle of Cheryl (see above) and grandfather of Lily (see below).

Lily Cole, 25-year-old beautiful model and actress whose photograph is often on the front of the Independent on Sunday's Style Magazine. Daughter of George, TV's Minder (not pictured).

Laura Ashley Cole, 64, iconic fashion designer, formerly married to burly, sausage-guzzling German Chancellor, Helmut Kohl (see below).

Old King Cole, 1864-year-old former Colchester-born King of East Mercia, famous for his pipe-smoking and his love of popular music, which has since been inherited by his descendant Cheryl Cole (see above).

SOCCER CLICHES UPDATED
with John And Ashley

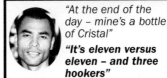

"At the end of the day – mine's a bottle of Cristal"

"It's eleven versus eleven – and three hookers"

"There are no easy games in the Premiership – but there are some easy women"

"It's a game of two halves: her top half and her bottom half"

"The lads literally ran their pants off"

"Football's coming home – to find me in bed with its girlfriend..."

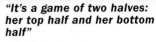

TV Highlights

Coming soon
The Se❌ Factor

ALL over the country young hopefuls are desperate to become the next footballer's bit on the side. But who has got what it takes to triumph as a world famous slapper? Join judge Ashley Cole as he auditions the young wannabes who are determined to live the dream, go on a journey and sell their story to Max Clifford. Will they have the Cheques Factor? (Surely "Sex Factor"? Ed.)

"Rapunzel, Rapunzel, let down your hair extensions!"

49

'NO EQUIPMENT SHORTAGE,' CLAIMS BROWN

by Our Defence Staff **Penny Pinch**

THE PRIME MINISTER, Mr Gordon Brown, angrily denied accusations from senior defence chiefs that there was a lack of suitable equipment being deployed in Afghanistan.

To Helmand and Back

"I felt completely safe at all times," he said, "and I had the use not only of a flak jacket but also a very nice helmet."

As he posed for pictures with British soldiers, he declared, "Look at those cameras! They are state of the art. And there are loads of them all functioning flawlessly in desert conditions. How dare anyone suggest that our brave boys are not being given the very best that technology can offer?"

The Prime Minister went on

As he flew in to Helmand to meet the troops, he pointed out that his plane from England and his helicopter to the front line had both worked "absolutely perfectly".

to promise that he would spend "whatever it took" to get onto the front pages.

Shot at dawn

"If the army asks me for support then of course I will be on the first plane out to deliver much needed visits."

Asked by one soldier if "this thing was winnable," he replied, "The election? Of course – particularly if I keep doing photo opportunities".

Government Unveils Replacement Vehicle for Snatch Land Rover

"Well, I hope it's a little girl, so we can dress it up and put on make up and make it look sexy and that"

Notes&queries

Why does the Afghan President Hamid Karzai wear that funny green carpet thing round his shoulders ?

(Mrs Ludmilla Monbiot)

● Karzai belongs to the ancient Afghan tribe of the Gheezas and comes from the mountainous Bakhanda region of Northern Afghanistan. Major Starborgling is quite wrong when he suggests that the Gheezas are warriors and Karzai a former warlord. The Gheezas, on the contrary, pride themselves on their capacity to avoid danger. They value, above all, cunning, guile and the skill to deceive even their friends. As for the green cloak, it is a throwback to the days when many of the Gheezas were carpet-sellers, famous for importing cheap, mass-produced carpets from Birmingham and selling

them at grossly inflated prices to unsuspecting foreign tourists.
E.O. St J. Sopwith, Barnstaple

Why is the legal high Mephedrone known as "Meow Meow"?

(Rebecca Wurridge)

● This drug was originally an ingredient used in the popular cat food "Pussychunx". The manufacturers deliberately introduced Mephedrone into the food, knowing it to be addictive to cats – thus ensuring that they refused other brands of cat food. The RSPCA brought an action against "Pussychunx", claiming that Mephedrone caused several degenerative disorders, as a result of which it was banned. Subsequently selling the drug to human beings, dealers continue to call it "Meow Meow" in imitation of the addicted cats' plaintive cries.
Dr T.S. McCavity, Pets 'R' Us, Bournemouth

● Dr McCavity must be taking Mephedrone if he believes the above load of catswallop."Meow Meow" is a corruption of "Mao Mao" and the drug is a powerful Kenyan herbal intoxicant made from the leaves of the Kenyatta tree. Members of the Mao Mao tribe were known to chew the drug before going into battle, believing it would render them immune from harm. It is, of course, entirely safe and I myself have been a user for many years with no ill effects at all.
Dave Mad, c/o The Priory

Answers please to the following:

Do worms sing? Who invented the asterisk? Has anyone read Martin Amis' new novel?

That Honorary Degree Citation In Full

SALUTAMUS KATERINA LETTE NOVELISTAM ANTIPODEAM FAMOSISSIMA PER JOCUNDIS SEXUALIS ET DOUBLOS ENTENDRIBUS REPETITIVIS EXEMPLI GRATIA 'CLITERATI' 'PUNNILINGUS' 'STIFF UPPER LABIA' ETCETERA ETCETERA PER MULTOS ANNOS FAVORITA GROUPIA RUMPOLI MORTIMERI (AVOCATO ET DRAMATICO CELEBRATUM) NUNC KATARINA EST HONORATA DOCTORI EPISTOLARUM IN TRIUMPHO FEMINISTA AUSTRALIENSIS SUPER PUBLICI SCHOLARI SNOBBI ANGLICI OXBRIDGIENSIS POOFTOS. GAUDEAMUS SHEILA BONUS-ON-YER SPORTA POSSUMENSIS!! GLADIOLIS MAXIMUS ET XXXX-OFFUS AD OMNES POMMIS BASTARDIS!!

© Southampton Solent University (formerly the Mission for Seamen) MMX

POLLY FILLER on Mother's Day

OK! It's official! I'm the best mum in the world and I've got the card to prove it! Toddler Charlie came up trumps on Sunday and brought a tear to his (yummy!) mummy's eye! And, you know, it makes it all worthwhile – all the juggling, all the worrying, all the guilt about being a working mum on the frontline of the trenches of modern parenthood! One little card proves that us wummies* are not psychologically damaging our kids, but instead bringing them up to be lively, independent, creative and loving toddlers.

And, you know what the best thing was, as I tried to tell the Useless Simon, as he sat slumped in front of Michael Winner's Extreme TV Dinners on E4 Plus Dave One, presented by Claudia Winkleman... forget it, sad Simon, she's way out of your league, even though with that fringe she looks like a fish... where was I?

OH, the best thing about Charlie's Mother's Day card was that he actually had gone to all the trouble of making the au pair go out and buy it for him! Bless! That's my boy! And thank goodness I didn't give Eczxploytia the weekend off to go and see *her* mother in Szplob.
© P. Filler.

As I call working mummies on my hilarious blog on wumsnet, soon to be turned into a motion picture (starring Carey Mulligan to play yours truly!).

"I really have to go, there's someone at the door"
TIM BALES

'THE BILL' TO BE ABOLISHED

by 'Old' Bill Deedes

The latest victim of the widespread government cutbacks is the once popular "Police Force".

The Bill as it is known to fans is to be discontinued after a run of nearly 200 years.

Said a spokesman "It is just not working any more. The public are fed up with the storylines which are always the same. You ring up the police, nothing happens, the end".

The police were unavailable for comment.

THE BOOK OF BENJAMIN

Chapter 94

1. And, lo, there was ruling in Israel in those days Benjamin, the son of Netanyahu.

2. And Benjamin looked upon Jerusalem and sayeth, "Let there be more dwellings for the sons and daughters of Israel – even upon the land that technically belongeth to the Arabites."

3. And it was even as he commanded.

4. But then there cometh to the land of Israel, a man sent by Obama, and he was called Biden, which is to say, "The President-is-too-busy-to-come-himself".

5. And Biden was an peacemaker who sayeth, "Why cannot the Arabites and the Israelites lieth down together even as the Lion and the Lamb

6. "Without the Lion smiting the Lamb and biting off its head?"

7. But, verily, whilst Biden was sitting down to break bread with Benjamin, there came an announcement.

8. A messenger arriveth saying to Biden, "Thou knowest thou asked us to do something about these dwellings?

9. "Lo, we have done. We have built lots more. Even an thousandfold."

10. And Biden waxed wroth and gnashed his teeth saying, "Cursed are you Benjamin! For I have come amongst you and you have repaid with me with betrayal.

11. "You are as an viper that lurketh in the deserts of Hebron that striketh the toad in the noon day sun when his back is turned away."

12. But Benjamin laughed him to scorn, saying, "Truly I say unto you, we regret the timing of the announcement which was most unfortunate but sadly it is too late to stop the dwellings going up.

13. "Get thee stuffed, even as the olive is stuffed with the anchovy in the groves of Judea that have now been taken over from the Arabites."

14. And Biden departed in sorrow to his own land, drawing a line under the whole thing and declaring it was time to moveth on.

(Continued for ever)

A Taxi Driver writes

EVERY week a well-known ex-Minister talks openly into a concealed microphone about how he is prepared to do anything for money.

This week: **Steve Byers**
(cab-inet no. 173486)

So where's it to then, guv. House of Commons? House of Lords? All the same to me. You've struck lucky, guv. I know everyone and everywhere, and all the short cuts, know what I mean. Fancy Whitehall? I can get you in anywhere you like.

Look, Number Ten. Gordon Brown lives here, I know him well. I can get you five minutes with him. I'll put it on the meter. So, lets have a look, how are we doing? Oh, it's about ten grand

so far. I'm afraid that's the going rate these days. See that bloke up there on the column – that's Lord Nelson, very important man. Do you want to meet him? I can sort that for another five. So what have we got now? £15K? Why don't we call it £70 grand and I'll give you a receipt, then we can both claim it on expenses. Ok squire? Be lucky. I 'ad that Tony Blair in the back of the cab once. Very wealthy gentleman.

NEXT WEEK: Pat Hewitt gives you a tour of Britain's health trusts for only £100 grand.

"When the lights are on in my eyes, I'm for hire"

BANX

BBC Radio 3

Berlusconi's *Trial by Jury*, a one act comic opera

The curtain rises to find the beleaguered English advocate, Signor David Mills, in his prison cell where he faces a long term in jail for bribery and corruption. He sings the haunting aria *Tessa Dorma (The Jowell House Rock)*.

The door opens and the Robber Baron enters with good news. He explains that under a new law which he has just introduced all crimes committed by friends of the Robber Baron have "a sell-by date". And guess what! Mills' offences are "out of time" and he is free to go. There follows the triumphant duet *Siamo Coppeli di Crooki (We're Just a Couple of Innocent Men)*.

The two characters repair to the local tavern where they are entertained by a group of scantily clad hostesses, dental hygienists and weather girls, many of whom are hoping to stand for office in the forthcoming Italian regional elections. The chorus sing *Que Bello Mondo (What A Wonderful World)*.

'I CAN'T BELIEVE I'M NOT BUTTERFILL' — MP's shock tape

by Our Lobbygate Staff **Des Patches**

A VERY senior and important Tory MP who has never been heard of before, Sir Tufton Butterfill, has been secretly taped by Channel 4's Despatches trying to cash in on his political contacts for huge sums of money.

That Despatches Tape in full

Sir Tufton: I think I'm just the man you need. In fact your clients would be very well advised to snap me up before my daily rates go up... I'm what you'd call very much on the inside track... I'm the man who talked Dave Cameron into standing as leader... so he owes me one, if you know what I mean! I think your people would find it useful to meet the chap who's going to be the next prime minister... would I speak up a bit and look over towards that innocuous bag over there? Yes, certainly, my dear... now where was I? Oh

Lord Butterup

yes, everyone knows that when I step down from the Commons in a few week's time I'm going to be sent up to the 'other place' as Lord Bootsfill... and obviously that's going to change the picture considerably... because that's where all the business is done these days... I don't suppose you know that, but that's precisely the sort of inside stuff I'll be able to help you with... by the way, you've got to keep all this very much under your pretty little hat, because if the faintest word of this got out into the media, then my old friend Dave would have to do his whiter than white act and strike my name off the list. Do you fancy buying me lunch? The fish at the Mirabelle is awfully good.

PREZZA SEMPER MALAPROPUS

KenPyne

YES! IT'S LORD PRESCOTT

The Red Dragon Pursuivant, Sir Darcy Anstruther-Fitz-Barkworth, of the College of Heralds today revealed details of the coat of arms of the soon-to-be ennobled Baron Prescott of Humbug in the county of Yorkshire.

The shield is quartered and features two heraldic

jaguars, a pair of crossed croquet mallets on a field verde, a Deputy Prime Minister rampant on a secretary, and a clenched fist above the motto: "Prezza Semper Malapropus".

His wife is to be known as Lady Pauline Prescott of That Hairdo. (*Surely "Ilk", Ed.*)

They Shoot Horses Don't They...

THE STORY SO FAR: Charles and Camilla have gone out for a romantic wedding anniversary walk. Now read on...

by Dame Sylvie Krin

"**T**HIS heather thingie is awfully good, isn't it? The way it's all purple and everything."

Charles gazed across the sun-dappled waters of Loch Banham towards the Auld Hoose, his highland hideaway retreat on the Royal Balmooney estate.

"It's bloody cold, Chazza, isn't it? You must be freezing to death in that kilt and those wellies." Camilla trudged dutifully behind her husband, wishing she could dilute the chill Caledonian air with a drag on an unfiltered Old Sinbad Extra Strong Navy Shag. But, alas, such vices were now a distant memory. And the robust Prince Charles was undaunted.

"No, no. I'm warm as toast in the old McQueen tartan and my trusty Mitchell and Webb Highland striders."

Camilla shivered. "So long as you're all right, that's all that matters and... whoops!"

As she spoke these very words, Camilla lost her noble footing and fell heavily into the surrounding peat.

Charles turned and frowned. "I thought I told you to lay off the Old McHackey's Single Malt until we got back, didn't I?"

Camilla winced bravely. "I'm not pissed, Chazza. I've tripped over a bloody rabbit hole and I think I've broken my bloody leg."

"Which one?"

"I don't know. Rabbit holes all look the bloody same. For God's sake, do something."

Suddenly Charles snapped into action, instantly recalling all his training as a former First Aid Badge holder (2nd Class) in the Gordonstoun Scout Patrol.

"Right. You just keep very still and I'll sort this out."

"Thanks, Chazza. You're a brick."

She managed a weak smile and Charles glowed with a sense of worth and purpose that he felt so seldom nowadays amidst

all the constraints of his inactive life. Yes, it was what his old friend and mentor Laurens van der Post used to tell him on those long evenings around the campfire at Lake Terreblanche, when they discussed the whole meaning of life thingie. What was it the old sage had once said? "Everybody needs somebody to love." How true that was. How very, very true.

"**I**T'S alright darling, I'm back." Camilla looked up through the pain and saw that Charles had indeed returned.

"Have you brought help?" she asked, bravely fighting back the tears.

"You betcha, old girl. I've found some Damson nettles, some Dacrewort, some Grandad's Elbow, some Blearhazel and this yellow weed chap which cures everything. Now eat the nettles and I'll rub these other thingies on your leg. Just tell me where it hurts."

"There, I hope!" Camilla pointed to Charles' head and, summoning what little strength she had left, swung her Louis Walsh handbag at it, scoring a direct hit on the heir to the throne's cranium.

"Ow!"

"Now just call a bloody ambulance!"

THE Queen's Own Royal Air Ambulance took off over the deer-strewn slopes of Glenn Close, heading for the Abercrombie General A&E department. The cheery pilot, Captain Armstrong-Miller, turned to the recumbent Camilla, who had been made comfortable in the rear of the Wessex Ardent Helicopter.

"Don't worry, Ma'am, we'll have you plastered in no time."

"Good idea," agreed Camilla, unscrewing a silver hip flask (a gift from Sheikh Quoqtayl of the United Arab Petroleum States, engraved with the legend *"A wee dram afore we stone ye to death!"*). She took a healthy swig and sighed.

"That's better. This is the kind of alternative medicine that really works, eh Chazza?"

Charles looked gloomily out of the window as the spring sunshine was lost behind a looming cloud. A broken leg... a broken dream.

© Sylvie Krin 2010.

"You should have told me you only use off duty baggage handlers"

THEY'RE OFF!
THE EYE'S ELECTION TEAM

Bringing you all the latest news, views, comment and analysis from the hustings. Everything you need to know about Election 2010 – the ins, the outs, the highs, the lows, the gains, the gaffes, the winners, the losers, the polls, the trouser press (*Is this right. Ed?*) It's all here in the *Eye*. And here is the team!!

Phil Space
Space will follow the action round the clock and bring you up to the minute updates as they happen.

Glenda Slagg
Slagg will offer her analysis of what the leaders wives Sam and Sarah are wearing. Are you sick of them? Or do you love them? Glenda will decide. Geddit?

Dave Spart
Veteran Spart is the alternative voice to give you a different perspective on how utterly sickening and totally you know irrelevant the entire capitalist... er ...

Pattie O'Heater
Green champion O' Heater gives an environmental perspective on the parties and how they measure up to the challenge of global warming and follows in the carbon footprints of the main protagonists.

E.J.Thribb
The *Eye's* poet in residence writes a daily poem on one of the campaign issues. Today it's the proposed increase in National Insurance payments.

Sally Jockstrap
The *Eye's* sports correspondent gives a running commentary from the sidelines. Who will score a hole–in–one first? Who will get a home run over the net in the final? Sally is watching and getting it wrong as only Sally can.

Polly Filler
Polly Filler gives the all – important mums *Eye* view of the election. Will the working mothers go for Dishy Dave or will Gruff Gordon win the day? Polly has no idea.

A Cabbie
Vinnie Snozza, the *Eye's* resident cab driver considers all the parties and rejects them out of hand on the grounds that none of them promise to restore capital punishment.

Max Hitler Hastings
Hastings tells readers to "vote conservative".

Blog Trotter
The *Eye's* Ace webwatcher will be scouring the tweets, the blogs, the forums, looking for the latest on–line gossip, conspiracy and total rubbish.

Sir Peregrine Worstthorne
Veteran right of centre columnist will be asleep throughout the campaign and has asked not to be disturbed.

● *Whatever you do before May 6th, make sure your eye is on the Eye!*

ELECTION ROUND-UP

Election campaign which began three months ago begins

■ There was widespread joy throughout the Country today as an election campaign which began over three months ago began.

"Now instead of having to endure daily briefings from the party leaders, uncosted policy announcements and hideously misconceived poster campaigns attacking their opponents, we can now look forward to daily briefings from the party leaders, uncosted policy announcements and madly misconceived poster campaigns attacking their opponents".

Brown 'will have a role in campaign'

■ Labour Central Office has angered some party activists by confirming that Gordon Brown will have a role in the General Election campaign alongside his wife, Sarah.

"This strategy could easily backfire," said one worried party activist. "This election is all about what a strong powerful woman Sarah Brown is and we don't want to muddy that message with too many appearances by Gordon Brown."

Gordon Brown's role in the campaign has already been criticised by the leader of the Conservative Party, Samantha Cameron.

BBC coverage defended

■ The BBC Director General Mark Thompson has defended the BBC's coverage of the General Election after it was revealed that number of BBC staff involved is greater than the number of people eligible to vote in the election.

"I don't need to be told by the likes of you it's too large. If I decide it's too large, then I will appoint someone expensive to tell me so.

"Just getting ready for the General Election, mate"

WHAM BAM GLAM MAM SAM CAM IN PRAM SCAM HAM DAMN

(headline cont. p. 94)

'HE'S LOVELY – HE'S A REAL PUSSYCAT,' Says Mrs Nick Griffin

BNP Reveal Secret Weapon for Election

by Our Political Staff **Michael Whitesonly**

NOT TO be outdone by the wives of the three main party leaders, the British National Party is to promote Nick Griffin's wife Brunhilde during the forthcoming General Election campaign.

Brunhilde has given an hour-long interview to TV's Masterchef Greg Wallace in which she talks frankly for the first time about the BNP, her husband and his love of goldfish.

The interview is to be shown tonight on ITV and takes place in the Griffin's modest "Bunkerlow" in White City and provides extraordinary insights into the man who could well not become Britain's next Prime Minister.

Brunhilde tells Greg:

● *Nick is a loving husband and is terrific with the fish – Herman,*

Heinrich and Max Mosley.

● *Nick is a great romantic. When he proposed he went down on one knee and asked for proof that there were no darkies in my family.*

● *Nick is very keen on gardening. In fact, he wants to take over next door's garden as well to provide more "living room" for our fish.*

● *Nick does have his faults. He often leaves his black shirts lying on the floor for me to pick up and he always dumps his jackboots in the hall for me to fall over when I am going out to take the fish for a walk.*

● *Nick and I always go on holiday together. Last year we went to Austria (again) to visit our great friend David Irving in prison.*

(Interview in full p. 94)

"Looks like they're ready for government"

TORY HQ

ALL CORPORATE BACKHANDERS ACCEPTED

RSJ

BLAIR GOES ON SAFARI AS ELECTION CAMPAIGN STARTS

by Our Political Staff **Anji Hunter**

THE former Prime Minister Tony Blair has created a new controversy by setting off on old-fashioned hunting trip to Africa.

Said a spokesman, "Tony has gone to bag some money. He wants to collect the so-called Big Five, ie Five Million Dollars.

"If there is a killing to be made, Tony wants to do it."

But there were furious protests last night from conservationists. One of them said, "A lot of this money is endangered nowadays. It's very rare for cash of this size to be at liberty. And it's obscene that Tony has got it in his sights

just to have it stuffed into his bank account".

Safari Tip

Q: How do you tell an African elephant from a former leader of the Labour Party?

A: The African elephant has smaller ears and a trunk containing less money.

All aboard the Lib Dem Battlebus!

I look forward to meeting the voters

EXCLUSIVE TO ALL PAPERS

MAN OFF THE TV WHO USED TO SIT ON ONE SOFA WILL NOW SIT ON ANOTHER SOFA

"Oh blimey – I wish I hadn't eaten all that bread"

ON OTHER PAGES

● Picture of other man who used to sit on sofa on the telly who will now sit on a sofa on the telly that the other man isn't sitting on anymore.

● Picture of woman off the tv who also sits on sofa where the man off the telly used to sit and who now might sit on another sofa or might not.

Times Travel

Mary Ann Bighead

Why I was so clever to travel round the world with my children

It's four years on and a lot of you will probably have been wondering how clever the Bighead family are now – having had the experience of a mini-gap year.

Well the answer is... cleverer than ever – and certainly cleverer than you! Some people were doubtful as to the wisdom of removing our daughters from full-time education and heading off to the lush forests of Grosso Teto and the arid plains of Grande Cephalo in South America.

My daughter Brainella's headmistress for one, expressed her reservations about a four-year old being entrusted with sailing a 75ft schooner around the active volcano Vasticapo.

But guess what? It turned out that she was wrong and we were right. Perhaps that's why she's just a headmistress and I

write for the Times!

Anyway, the girls thrived and the whole experience expanded their minds hugely almost to the point where they could keep up with me. And it's borne fruit in so many ways.

Brainella, 8, now has no need for a gap year because she already knows everything. She is going straight to Oxford – as Chancellor. Intelligencia, 10, has seen so much of life that she has decided to start her career straight away – as a leading brain surgeon, rocket scientist and Nobel prize-winning geneticist, working at NASA's Institut d'Intelligence Supérieur in Kleverkloggen in Belgium.

So if you fancy taking some time out from the humdrum life you are leading – don't bother because the Bighead family has already done it much more successfully than you could ever do!

© *Mary Ann Bighead*

WHAT YOU WON'T READ IN THE MURDOCH PRESS

IT'S THE SON WOT LOST IT!

by Our Political Staff **Rebekka Wadesin**

YES, HE'S bonkers! It's official! Rupert's nutty nipper, James, went beserk when he read in the snooty Independent newspaper that his Dirty Digger Dad, 94, was trying to influence the election and telling the readers to vote for Cameron.

Journalists at the nobby news-sheet were open-mouthed when Sonny Jim, along with Wacko Wade, the self-styled terror of the Paedos, stormed into their office and erupted in a foul-mouthed tirade which would make Gordon Ramsay blush.

Off His Trolley

"It was like something out of The Sopranos," said one shocked journo, Roger Alton. "That sort of language isn't acceptable in this day and age."

In the end, the Independent's editor was forced to call the police after Mad Mini Murdo started issuing bizarre threats, shouting, "If you accuse my dad

of running everything, I'll get him to close you down".

Shames Murdoch

The Indie's editor, Mr Simon Kellner, was said to be in a stable condition last night, following counselling for Post-Murdoch Traumatic Disorder.

"He can barely bring himself to redesign the newspaper," said a worried friend.

That Victoria line in full

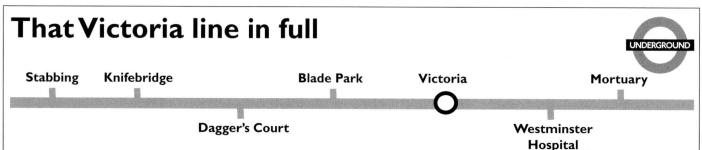

A Message from Lord Gnome

IT IS with a degree of reluctance that I add my signature to the list of Britain's distinguished business leaders who have voiced their opposition to the proposed increase in National Insurance.

Eminent signatories include such influential figures as Sir Monty Greed, Chairman of Greed Garden Centres (Weybridge), Lord Kwikfit, the Chairman of World of Carpets (Nuneaton), and Sir Stavros Moussaka, CEO of the no frills airline Flybynite (Luton to Limoges £1.99, use of toilet extra).

Our concern in this matter is purely to preserve vital jobs at a difficult and dangerous time for the British economy when all of us in the business community are experiencing the effect of the global downturn.

It would be entirely wrong and possibly libellous to suggest that any of the above, including myself, have been motivated to intervene in this debate by a desire not to pay any more money to the government with the resultant potential drop in our emoluments.

Yours patriotically,
LORD GNOME,
Chairman Accupunctura
(formerly World of Leather, Barrow-in-Furness)

"It'll be interesting to see how the markets react to this"

GUARDIAN ELECTION SPECIAL

Top Feminist Totty's Love Romps with Randy Italian Romeo – EXCLUSIVE

The famous Italian film director, Frederico di Fellatio, known for such cinematic masterpieces as "La Dolce Vita Sackville West", "8½ out of 10 Cats", and "Carry on Casanova" *(surely "Casablanca"? Ed.)* once met the distinguished feminist icon and *Guardian* columnist Germaine Defoe. "Our eyes met across a crowded studio," she writes in G2, "and he uttered the immortal words, 'Hallo baby-doll, you fancy a quick (cont. p. 94)

FRUITY GIRL CLIMBS TO TOP OF NEWS AGENDA

by Our Mountaineering Staff **Ben Nevis**

Gratuitous picture

A FRUITY girl made history yesterday when she successfully reached the front pages of the highest circulation newspapers in Britain.

The girl, who is very fruity, was delighted by her epic achievement and told nobody, "I have very little experience when it comes to mountains of copy but I just climbed Everest and did my best to look as fruity as possible."

One hardened Fleet Street editor wept openly when the news came through.

"It makes you proud to be British. At last we have a 22-year-old mountaineer who has scaled the peaks of fruitiness and planted a story right at the top of the page."

Said fellow mountaineer Sir Ranolph Fiennes (not pictured because he's old and not fruity), "Hats and toes off to Fruitella!"

And another one

NOT COMING SOON

Bond isn't back in DR NO FILM

Yes! It's a race against time! Can Bond stop a plot by evil accountants to destroy the entire francise? Bond is called in by M (GM) and told his licence to make money has been revoked. Instead, he goes to see Q who equips him with the latest Walther PP45. "Pay attention", he says, "it looks like a boring piece of paper, but in fact it can kill you off completely." Is this the end?

CAST IN FULL

James Junk Bond	**Daniel Craig**
Miss Nomoneypenny	**Samantha Junk Bond**
M (GM)	**Dame Judi Debt**
Nojob	**Henry Blofeld**
Q (at JobCentre)	**John Close**
Man with the Golden Handshake	**Auric Goldman Sachs**
The Junk Bond Girls	**Plenty O'Creditors, Busty Flush & Kissy Goodbye**

(Produced by Cubby Brokelli)

'Clegg Now Bigger Than Jesus,' Say Beatles

by Our Political Staff
St John Lennon, St Paul McCartney and St George Harrison

IT'S OFFICIAL. Lib Dem leader Nick Clegg is now more popular than Winston Churchill, Barack Obama and Jesus Christ, the founder of the religion that was called after him.

Totally unknown two days ago, the charismatic Mr Clegg is now, according to the latest polls, the most admired figure in Britain today, an astounding 70 percent ahead of the Queen and a staggering 12 percent ahead even of Joanna Lumley.

Vince Cable TV

Clegg owes his stratospheric rise to one of the most astonishing performances ever seen on a television screen.

He stunned millions of viewers with the breath-taking skill by which he:

● called people by their first names

● looked straight into the camera.

Within minutes, phone lines were jammed by half the country pledging to devote their lives to following the man

they described as their new spiritual leader.

Said one awed convert, "He's fresh, he's young, he's not like the others – except that he is".

Right across the country the story was the same.

St Nick

Toddlers from Totnes, teenagers from Teeside, pensioners from Preston all joined together, singing hymns of praise for the man they call "the Moderate Messiah".

But who is he, this secular saviour of a broken Britain who could soon be storming into Number Ten on the greatest landslide ever seen in British or any other politics?

The answer is that Clegg is totally different from the normal politician. He was educated at Westminster School, the son of a banker and he has never had a job outside politics. All this marks him out as *(cont. p. 94)*

Mid-Lie Crisis

"I promise that we will er... er... er..."

K.J.Lamb

THE Sun
Friday, April 30, 2010

Cameron wins TV Debate and Grand National page 94

IS CLEGG A POOF?

by Our Political Editor **James Murdoch**

HAILED by millions as the best thing since sliced bread, Lib Dem leader Nick Clegg may not be all that he seems, the Sun can reveal.

An in-depth Sun investigation has unearthed a number of highly disturbing facts about the so-called new Superman of British politics. Clegg:

● **leads a party formerly headed by Jeremy Thorpe who was gay**

● **attended a top public school – need we say more?**

● **looks young and** boyish and openly appeared on TV wearing make-up

● **is a close friend of Vince Cable who makes no secret of his love of ballroom dancing. Suspicious or what?**

Short of admitting that he is a big Judy Garland fan what more proof do the electorate need that Clegg is a secret gay?

Not that there's anything wrong with that of course – but do you really want him running your country?

Vote Conservative and keep our toddlers safe!

CLEGG FACTS

● Many of Clegg's relatives are foreign

● For many years Clegg worked as a secret agent for Col. Gaddafi and might well have been the Lockerbie bomber

● Clegg openly boasts that he once set fire to some very rare cacti and yet he claims to have a "green" agenda

● Clegg is going to keep the Tories out of power unless we can find some better dirt than this

© Murdochsmearinternational

The Daily Torygraph

Friday, 30 April 2010

CROOKED CLEGG IN EXPENSES SHOCK

Dodgy Lib Dem Claimed £1.39 For A Boots Own-Brand Toothbrush

By Our Political Staff
Andrew Killiklegg

FAR FROM being the whiter-than-white politician that he claimed in the TV Leaders' Debate, the Daily Torygraph can reveal that Nick Clegg is one of the worst expense fiddlers in the entire House of Commons.

The £1.39 toothbrush is shocking, but there are worse revelations to come, including a luxury biscuit worth over 25p.

But the Daily Torygraph has also discovered that Clegg has openly accepted financial donations from rich businessmen. What a disgrace! What other Party would even think of *(You're fired. Ed.)*

Daily Mail

FRIDAY, APRIL 30, 2010

VOTING FOR CLEGG WILL GIVE YOU CANCER – AND CAUSE COLLAPSE IN HOUSE PRICES

by Our Political Staff **Quentin LettsvoteTory, Stephen Tory-Glover** and **Peter O'Boresonabouthowawfultheotherpartiesare**

A SHOCKING new report has revealed that voting Liberal Democrat in the forthcoming General Election will immediately lead to the onset of terminal cancer.

The link between supporting the third party in the ballot and death is now beyond doubt and medical experts are urging people not to vote Lib Dem "if they wish to stay alive".

Vote Clegg – Get Cancer

One of the leading specialists who compiled the report, Dr Dacre, told the Mail, "You will die if you choose Clegg. This is a fact. You cannot say you have not been warned."

But the news gets worse. Not only will all Lib Dem voters suffer a painful death but, by their irresponsible behaviour, they will cause a meltdown in the British housing market.

Said property expert, Mr Dacre of leading estate agents Dacre, Paul and Dacre, "With all these dead Lib Dem voters there will be a glut of empty properties on the market. This will cause a catastrophic fall in house prices."

Lib Doom

He continued, "We estimate that an average family house will drop in value by over 200% – meaning most home-owners will be in negative equity and will have their houses repossessed leading to mass suicides which will of course further depress the housing market."

The message is clear. Not only is Nick Clegg a Nazi and very possibly Hitler's secret love child (*see yesterday's Mail*) but he is the Angel of Death and (cont. p. 94.)

ON OTHER PAGES: "Coloured Daleks – coming over here and taking our jobs" – claims ordinary Dalek.

THOSE TOP ELECTION SLOGANS IN FULL

Vote **CLEGG** .... *Get* **CAMERON!**

Vote **BROWN** .... *Get* **MILIBAND!**

Vote **CAMERON** .... *Get* **CAMERON!**

Vote **GRIFFIN** .... *Get* **SENT HOME!**

Vote **MANDELSON** .... *Get* **YOU!**

Vote **MICHAEL CAINE** .... *Get* **CARTER!**

Vote **PRESCOTT** .... *Get* **STUFFED!**

HOW THE SECOND TV DEBATE TURNED NASTY

by Our Media Staff **Phil Inname**

AFTER the pleasantries of the opening BBC debate, this time at Sky the gloves were off and the three party leaders tore into each other like rabid rottweilers. It was savage, brutal and bruising – 90 minutes of bare-knuckled barbarism that set the election on fire.

Those highlights in full

Round One

Clegg: I just don't think that is right on immigration.

Brown: You're entitled to your opinion, Nick.

★ *Verdict*: *First Blood Brown*

Round Two

Clegg: I'm sorry but I think we think we need a comprehensive defence review.

Cameron: We suggested that ages ago, Nick.

★ *Verdict*: *Clegg on the Ropes*.

Round Three

Clegg: I think we need to restore public confidence in politics.

Brown: You two are just like Punch and Judy fighting over the sausages except the crocodile has already eaten them, smile and try not to look weird. Oh, I shouldn't have read that bit out.

★ *Verdict*: *Knockout blow to Brown*.

'I BELIEVE IN CLEGG,' Confesses Dawkins

by Our Religious Staff **The Rev. A.N. Wislon**

THE world's best-known atheist Prof. Richard Dawkins has shocked his thousands of followers across the world by announcing that he now believes that Nick Clegg is the Messiah, capable of saving the world.

"I admit," he said, "that there is no scientific evidence for the existence of such an omnipotent and benign being as Clegg. But these are matters of belief, not of rational proof.

"I personally feel that Clegg is all around us, holding out the promise of a better life and a better world, if we will only have the courage to follow him.

"It's silly to think of this wonderful Supreme Being as an old man with a long white beard. That was his predecessor, Ming Campbell."

Prof. Dawkins concluded by lashing out at non-believers from the lack-of-faith community.

"I mean, if you don't agree with me, you must be some kind of gullible superstitious nutcase."

Prof. Dawkins will be signing copies of his *Why I Am Always Right* at the LibDem Bookshop, Market Barkworth on Thursday 11 September.

"What do I say to the people who say I can't ad-lib?"

Notes&queries

VOLCANO SPECIAL

What is the correct pronunciation of the Icelandic volcano Eyjafjallajökull??

(Standish Walmart, Stevenage)

● Mrs Godbat is quite wrong when she says that the final two syllables remain silent and that the main emphasis should be on the third syllable. As we can see from the famous passage in the great 11th century epic, the Agasaga, describing an earlier eruption of this volcano in 923, the closing syllables represent the name of a much-feared troll who was imprisoned beneath the glacier by the 'lava god', Magma Magmasson. It is therefore particularly important that the last two syllables should be emphasised and pronounced to rhyme with the name of the German Chancellor, Merkel.
E Trimfittering, Purfleet

Why is it unsafe for aircraft to fly through volcanic ash?

(Olbas Onanugu)

● Your readers have been misled by the explanation given by government scientists. Their suggestion that small particles of volcanic dust might enter the internal ducting of jet engines, heating them to millions of degrees Celsius, thus causing the plane to explode, is a serious exaggeration. As was made clear by the official inquiry carried out by Lord Duckworth following the celebrated Nornet NO294 incident in 1989, volcanic dust poses no threat whatever to aircraft and in fact can make a useful contribution to fuel efficiency by acting as micro-inducers in the fuel injection process. I write this in my personal capacity and not of course as part of my role as head of public relations for British Airways.
Barry Cheese

Since I and my wife have now been stuck in Lansoprazole for two weeks, will my travel insurance pay for our accommodation, or should my claim be against the airline, or indeed the travel company with which we booked?

(Derek and Judy, surname withheld, Tring)

● This is a 'grey' area. It depends very much on what type of travel insurance you are covered by. Take my own case, for instance. I went to a family wedding in the Greek island of Kosmos and found to my horror that our airline, Flybynite, had grounded all its fleet for a fortnight and were only offering in compensation a one-euro-a-day voucher to pay for all our subsistence. Naturally, being British, we all got together to hire a local fishing boat belonging to Iannis Kostapaketos, who ferried us to the mainland, where we hired a taxi which drove us the 1500 miles to Sofia in Bulgaria, where we were lucky enough to get on the last train to Salzburg, where we were fortunate enough to find two second-hand bicycles for sale at a cost of €700 each. Within days we had reached the French coast where the good old Royal Navy had promised to take us home. Sadly, they did not arrive but a group of us were undaunted and managed to negotiate the hire a small foot-propelled craft from the excellent firm of *Pedalos Sont Nous*. After 27 days of stalwart pedalling, we sighted the coast of Somaliland. Imagine our disappointment when were taken prisoner by pirates. We were even more disappointed when our insurance company flatly refused to pay out the £1 million ransom demanded by our captors. Let this be a warning to all your readers not to put any trust in insurance policies until they have read the small print.
The Mancroft family (whereabouts unknown)

HUGE ASHCROFT CLOUD COVERS BRITAIN

by Our Political Staff **Quentinletsvotetory**

A HUGE cloud of cash was reported to be floating over the United Kingdom, particularly affecting marginal areas.

Said a worried observer, "This cash is making it very difficult to operate electoral machinery in a normal way. The money gets everywhere, clogging things up or, in some cases, clegging them up, which wasn't the idea at all, and *(cont. p. 94)*

"There now, everything that was really lethal is now really, really safe"

MET OFFICE

mikewilliams.

UNBEATABLE COALITION DEAL!

Vote for one party...

...and get one free!

'We've Seen It All Before'

Writes Alan Watneys

THERE is nothing new about a so-called hung parliament, a phrase that was originally coined by the late E.P. Snell, the legendary political editor of the Morning Sketch, to describe the events of 1924 when Lloyd George was unable to form a government and was forced to make overtures to the then leader of UKIP, Sir Nigel Cholmondeley-Farrago, whose fledgling party had scored a notable success in a recent by-election in Barkworth North where they had come a credible last against strong opposition from Sir Oswald Mosely's resurgent Marmite Referendum Party (the MRP). And, talking of hung parliaments, younger readers will remember the events of 1974 when Sir Edward Heath, as he then was, approached Liberal leader Jeremy Thorpe with the words "Hello, Sailor". *(Is this right? Ed.)* So there is nothing new about a hung parliament or indeed about this column which I first wrote in 1887 and *(cont. p. 94)*

DAILY ✠ EXPRESS
THE WORLD'S GREATEST NEWSPAPER

FRIDAY APRIL 30, 2010

CLEGG WILL ALLOW FOREIGN VOLCANOS IN BRITAIN

By our Conspiracy Staff
Phillipa Front-Page

EXPERTS today warned that Nick Clegg's astonishing poll figures were certain to plummet after it was revealed that, under Liberal Democrat immigration policy, there would be nothing to stop Icelandic volcanoes settling in Britain.

"These volcanoes have made our life an utter misery, yet the Liberal Democrats want these volcanoes to settle in Britain. Why?", asked the Conservative leader David Cameron as he walked across the Channel to rescue stranded British tourists and *(cont. p. 94)*

ELECTION TOO CLOSE TO CALL

by Our Poetry Staff **JOHN BETJAMONEY**

Oxford, Tuesday

THE CITY of dreaming spires was last night being swept by what they are calling "Thribbmania", following a sensational performance by the youthful Eye versifier at a public poetry reading.

All the main candidates had appeared in front of the voters (Sid and Doris Day-Lewis) to recite examples of their work.

First Past The Poets

Thribb electrified his audience with his newly-minted ode *So. Farewell then the old poetry*, in which he promised a wholly new approach to poetry, which he said had been destroyed by the "tired clichés" of what he called "the clapped-out old hacks of yesteryear".

"People are desperate for a change," said Thribb. "We don't have to do it in the same old way. I'm offering change. I'm offering hope. I'm offering a vision of a better Britain with better poetry for everyone."

An on-the-spot poll taken after the meeting showed a pro-Thribb swing from zero to 90 percent.

E.J. Thribb is 17½.

That Oxford Poetry Election In Full

Who are they, the men vying for poetry's number one hot seat?

Reginald Bunting, 72, previously the odds-on favourite before the rise of Thribbmania, has published over three slim volumes of verse in the past 50 years. His collection, *Klaxos,* was runner-up for the Gold Palm of Romania Award in 1953. He lives quietly in the Suffolk village of Lymeswold.

Mike Horrormaskovich, 75, beatnik and inventor of Slamdunk poetry and former editor of the seminal 70s' poetry magazine *Dead End*. Best known for his 18,000-page epic *Homage To West Bromwich Albion* and for playing the kazoo on the Today programme.

Roger Curmudgeonly, 53, is the anti-poetry candidate who is only standing to get his name into the papers. Curmudgeonly is best-known for his 600-page biography of the Dad's Army star Ian Lavender, entitled *Don't Tell Them Your Name, Pike.*

Sir Cleveland Jaws, 86, veteran TV personality and royal versifier. "This election is a farce," says Australian-born Jaws. "I refuse to stand in a silly election. Next time I hope I will get the job by public acclamation, which is what happened when Verlaine stood against Baudelaire in the legendary 1871 shoot out at the OK Corral."

"No, it's not safe for me to operate at these concentrations of dust"

LAST EVER PRIME MINISTERIAL DECREE

From the Bunker of the Supreme Leader

Comrades,

I salute you all on this glorious morning when we celebrate our historic victory in the recent election.

There were those who prophesied disaster for your Supreme Leader – they have been confounded as, with one voice, the nation cried out for the wise, strong and principled leadership given to them over the last three prosperous and successful years of my administration.

They recognised that only one man had the experience and the strength of character to lead them through the troubled waters and volcanic ash that threaten to destroy our economy. The public were not hoodwinked by the vacuous promises of the Neo-Conservative-Bullingdonian-Goveist-Cameronite-Osbournista jackals. No, they could see that beneath the sheep's clothing of Bodenist casual wear lay the Thatcherite wolves who would devour the entrails of the hard-working British Comrades and their hard-working families as they go about the country looking for work.

No, the figures speak for themselves. Cameron got a humiliating 36% of the vote, leaving a massive majority of the country rejecting his Old-Etonian-Top-Hattism.

Compare this with my overwhelming 29% in the polls!

You do not need to be a mathematical genius to see that if you turn those numbers round, it becomes 92% – a level of support unprecedented in the long history of our glorious party.

That is why, in accordance with constitutional precedents, I remain Supreme Leader – because that is my duty to the British people who have spoken so decisively. They have said that they want a change and I am the man to provide that change.

And, Comrades, let us at this point salute the great patriotic leader Comrade Clegg whose tiny but honest and well-meaning band of idealists came such a credible third despite the onslaught of the craven, drink-sodden hacks of the rotting corpse of Neo-Imperialist-Murdochism.

I have, as you know, long championed the cause of electoral reform. As long ago as yesterday, I made it clear that this is my number one priority in government. I want a system where the smaller parties, such as my own, are guaranteed at least one seat in the Prime Minister's chair.

Comrade Clegg is too wise to be seduced by the wiles of the Goveist claque and, in due course, will come to his senses and realise that **we** are his natural allies and only the Supreme Leader will recognise his extraordinary talents by giving him a leading role in my new government in any of the three vital posts listed below:

- Minister for Paperclips (Regions)
- Czar Czar – overseeing all the other Czars in the government
- Canteen Manager
- Minister Without Portfolio (or Job)

Then Comrade Clegg and I can lead the country to a new and brighter future where senior Comrades will all have a free windfarm in luxury care homes and every baby will have free broadband and lifelong tax credits plus a free iPad on which they can watch England's hard-working comrade footballers win the World Cup or at least come a poor second like I did...

(At this point, the Supreme Leader was advised by his medical supervisors to lie down and to take a potentially lethal dose of his medication – 100 Millibands of Bonkazapam)

Last Message from Comrade Lord Mandelson

May I be the first to salute the Supreme Leader on his notable victory. I know I speak for all Comrades in offering my heartfelt congratulations on his personal success at the polls. And what could be more appropriate if, at this moment of his greatest triumph, the Supreme Leader were to step down and make way for a younger successor who could capitalise on his enormous achievements. It is not for me to recommend who that person might be – indeed, were I to suggest, say, David Miliband for the job, it would be entirely inappropriate.

But Comrades will be well advised not to consider the discredited and aptly-named Comrade Balls, but to choose Miliband and to remember that I know where they all live.

Last Message from Comrade Alastair Campbell

Well, Comrades – what a f***ing shambles that was! Fancy losing to that chinless wonder Cameron and his bunch of toffee-nosed w**kers! If I'd been there from the start, we'd have kicked sh*t out of them!

THE BROON-ITES — THE CRAZY CELTS CRASHING OOT OF TH' COMMONS! — Fountain and Jamieson

GRR! HOW DARE THOSE SCUNNERS MAKE A SHADY DEAL TAE DECIDE WHO'S GAIN' TAE LEAD TH' COUNTRY! IT'S A SCANDAL, TH' NOO!

AYE! I CAN IMAGINE CAMERON AND CLEGG NOO, MEETING IN SOME PONCY RESTAURANT...

WORKIN' OOT SOME DODGY AGREEMENT ON A BACK OF A NAPKIN...

WHIT DID WE SAY?

EXIT

HENRY DAVIES

The New Coalition Academy

(formerly Brown's Comprehensive)

Headmaster: **David Cameron MA (Oxon)** Deputy Headmaster: **Nicholas Clegg MA (Cantab)**

A Message From the Headmaster

And a big hullo to all the staff, parents and children making up the new community that I call "The Big School"!

And, by the way, that big hullo comes equally from me, as your new headmaster, and my good friend and colleague, Nick Clegg, the new Deputy Prime Minister, who is sitting at the same desk with me as I write!

Is there something you'd like to say, Nick?

Nick says that he agrees with everything I've put in this letter so far! And that's how it's all going to work from now on.

The Old Brown's Comprehensive was all too obviously failing the community.

Standards had collapsed. The school had run out of money. And ideas! It was time for a fresh start.

That is why Nick and I were called in from our former posts, with the idea that we should pool our two teams to get **this** school firmly back on track.

Our first move has been to change the name, to symbolise the fact that this is a wholly new type of school.

And we have got rid of the old, dingy red uniforms, replacing them with a new combination of both of our colours.

So, from today, you can order the smart new blue and yellow striped blazers and ties on line at our new Parents Portal www. cleggcam.co.alition.uk (just click on *"Buy two blazers, Get tie free"* – Oh, and thanks for reminding me, Nick... there will be no charge for parents of more modest incomes, eg, earning less than £10,000 a year).

Let's be frank. A lot of people are already saying that this very exciting new project won't work. We say, it has to work, and it will work. It's in the interests of the school – and surely that has to be the main thing.

Nick is nodding his head vigorously as I write this. Thanks, Nick.

The point is that, although Nick and I come from different traditions – I'm probably a little bit more conservative and he's a little bit more liberal – when it comes down to it, we've got much more in common than people realise.

We're both the same sort of age. We have similar backgrounds educationally. We are both lucky enough to have lovely supportive wives who are prepared to muck in for the good of the school.

And, most importantly, neither of us has much experience in running a school, which is a tremendous advantage when you are a passionate believer in change and trying to

Two heads are better than one: *Dave and Nick address parents in the Headmaster's Garden*

do something new – which we both are.

I popped my head into the staff room just now – as Nick did – and you could sense the real feeling of excitement as our teams were getting to know each other.

Honestly, I couldn't really tell which of them were my team and which were Nick's – apart, of course, from poor old Mr Cable, the new head of our business studies department, who is sitting in a corner looking rather grumpy.

But then he is getting on a bit, and it's harder for older people to adjust to the new learning environment. I know that there aren't a lot of women teachers, and some parents are unhappy about that.

But at least we've made a really good start, with Mrs May and the delightful young Mrs Warsi (a moslem single mother, for those of you who think I'm some sort of out-of-touch public school figure, which I'm not, and neither is Nick!).

So what are our most urgent priorities as we start the first new term of this new era in the school's history?

First, we've got to sort out the school's finances, which I have to tell you are in a far worse state than we ever imagined.

I'm afraid our new bursar, Mr Osborne (George, as he wants everyone to call him), has got pretty bad news and whoever it was who left a note in the Bursary saying, *"There is no money left, ha ha ha!"*, should be ashamed of themselves. I've got a pretty good sense of humour and so has Nick, but this particular prank was not funny and not clever and this sort of behaviour will have no place in the school from now on.

Things are pretty serious. As from next term, all parents are going to have to dig deeply into their pockets to help us get through the tough times – to the tune of quite a few million pounds.

And there are going to have to be quite a few cuts in the school's many running expenses.

And yes, there will inevitably be some painful decisions for us about which facilities may have to be closed down.

Let me assure you that Mr Osborne and his new assistant Mr Laws are working flat out in their shirtsleeves as I write, to ensure that any cuts do not affect those school activities which we all most value.

So the rumour that the school nurse is only going to be coming in on alternate Wednesdays are completely untrue. It will be Tuesdays, once a fortnight.

But you can't expect Nick and I to turn the place around overnight. We're looking at a whole spreadsheet of options for cuts and savings. So watch out for the following:

● **a 20 percent upward revision in the price of school dinners**

● **the selling off of part of our playing fields for much-needed luxury housing developments.**

● **the closing down of the IT department and the school intranet system (which never worked anyway)**

● **the removal of the CCTV cameras from the boys' toilets**

● **the scrapping of the planned ID swipe cards which, apart from being hugely expensive, would have been – Nick tells me – the greatest infringement on pupils' liberties since the Great Reform Act of 1832.**

(And now it's my turn to nod my head in agreement with Nick!)

Anyway, that's quite enough for the first week. Nick and I have got some serious work to be getting on with, such as where to place all the wind turbines in the school's new "Eco-Zone" (formerly the headmaster's garden).

Yours in partnership,

Dvid & Nick

MASSIVE SWING TO ETON

THE CLEAR winner of the 2010 general election was the Windsor-based public school Eton College, which increased its representatives from 15 to 20 in an incredible late surge to the OE party.

One of the successful candidates, Jacob Rees-Mogg, led his supporters in a triumphant chant of "Moggie! Moggie! Moggie! In! In! In!"

Sadly, it was a different story for his sister Annunziata Rees-Mogg, where the crowd jeered, "Moggie! Moggie! Moggie! Out! Out! Out!"

NEW THIRD-PAST-THE-POST SYSTEM

We lost – now go back to your constituencies and prepare for Government!

The main thing is to concentrate on the debt...

Yes, you owe me big time

DO OSBOs WORK?

by Our Social Affairs Staff
Polly Toryboy

THE controversial system of attempting to control feral young people by administering an OSBO (Oxford Socialite Behavioural Order) has been called into question after the case of an out-of-control youth called "George" caused massive controversy across Britain.

"George" (his real name) was running around the country causing enormous embarrassment to the Conservative Party when the authorities served him with an OSBO, hoping to keep him off the streets and out of sight until after the election.

Now "George" is free again and has started appearing on television, talking about the economy and scaring members of the public with vague threats about making "cuts" and "taking all your money".

"The OSBO hasn't worked," said one terrified voter. "These short-term measures are no good if George simply comes back and starts reoffending everyone.

"It's time to tackle the root of the problem and make Vince Cable chancellor."

DAILY TELEGRAPH | Friday, 14 May 2010

Letters to the Editor

SIR – Now that the election dust has at last begun to settle, may I take this opportunity to correct one widespread misunderstanding perpetrated during the campaign by Mr Clegg and his many followers. Repeatedly we heard these young Johnnie-come-latelies, still wet behind the ears, claiming that the Liberals were somehow a "young" and "new" party, in contrast to the "tired old" Labour and Conservative Parties.

As someone who joined the Liberal Party in 1895, in response to Mr Gladstone's Newcastle Programme, I feel well qualified to put the record straight. The Liberal Party can indeed proudly claim to be older than the other two parties put together. It was founded in 1743 as the "Whig and Pen Society", taking its name from the well-known Fleet Street coffee house patronised by the likes of Addison, Steele and a young William Deedes.

The Tory Party is, comparatively, a puny stripling, having been launched only in 1834 as the Bullingdon Club. The Labour Party, as we all know, is even younger, having been formed in 1994 by an idealistic young clergyman, the Rev Tony Blair.

So, much as I admire Mr Clegg's enthusiasm and his undoubted charisma, his lamentable ignorance of the distinguished history of his own party renders him unfit for the highest office.

How much better for the party's fortunes it would have been, had they retained the services as their leader of the venerable 2000-year old Chinaman, Sir Ming Campbell. Inscrutable he may have been, but at least he did not make elementary mistakes like Mr Clegg.

Sir Jeremiah Thorpe-Gussett
The No Reform Club, Pall Mall.

THOSE COALITION CUTS IN FULL

1. The North of England
2. The 1922 Committee
3. Any policies we can't agree on

THE CROCODILE AND I HAVE FORMED AN IRREMOVABLE COALITION AND WILL SHARE THE SAUSAGES IN PERPETUITY...

RGJ

"I think I actually preferred the old-style Punch and Judy Politics"

The Lessons of the Cumbrian Tragedy

Hard to believe… beautiful summer's day… rural idyll… close-knit community… stunned… how could it happen… no warning… inexplicable horror… quiet village streets… trail of terror… no easy explanation… bound together… in the grief… hearts go out… thoughts and prayers… rallying round… coming to terms… return to normality… There's no way I can keep this up for 12 pages. Can't I do the World Cup instead? *(No, keep going, Ed)*

WHY DID THIS SEEMINGLY NORMAL, WELL-LIKED FAMILY MAN GO ON A RAMPAGE OF DEATH?

We don't know.

On Other Pages

● *"What drove me to write this piece?"* Top criminologist Dr Phil Boots asks himself why he fired off 5,000 words about Derrick Bird. Was it financial worries? Jealousy of other criminologists? A desire to be famous, even if only for churning out speculative rubbish? **2**

● *"Profile of a killer"* Profiler Maddie Tupp reveals that Bird was a totally normal weird, gregarious, solitary, brooding, fun-loving, one of the lads loner, seething with anger in an easy-going way **3**

● *"Why can't the media leave the local people alone?"*, asks Ian Trusive, reporting exclusively from Cumbria for the next fortnight **4**

More stories, more pix, even fewer excuses 5-94

PHARAOH TO SELL PYRAMID

by Our History Staff **Nile Ferguson**

THE legendary Pharaoh, King Fug, has stunned the world of Egypt by selling the luxury pyramid to a group of Arab traders.

The Pyramid has long been an attraction for tourists who flock to it in the hope of taking home a bargain.

Pyramid of Shops

But critics of the sale maintain that there is a curse associated with the pyramid known as 'The Curse of Fug'.

Said one, "Whoever owns the Pyramid will never get a British passport. He will end up old and mad, claiming to be Scottish and accusing the Duke of Edinburgh of murdering Princess Diana."

Pyramid Selling

Said the Pharaoh, "I have sold the Pyramid for one and a half billion shekels which is a fuggin' good deal.

"I hope the new owners will respect my wishes to be buried in the fuggin' Food Hall along with the Melton Mowbray Pork Pies and Portugese Rosé wine – 20% off in the fuggin' sale."

I'm still going to have a hands-on role

Watch out, girls!

"And, to recapitulate, here are the six key points my wife doesn't understand, again…"

That Religious Education GCSE Exam In Full

1. Who are the parents of the baby in the picture?
a) Wayne and Colleen
b) Ant and Dec
c) Richard and Judy

(20 marks)

Large Parts Of Athens In Ruins As Greeks Take To The Streets

by Our Man On The Acropolis **John Homer Simpson**

THE BIRTHPLACE of democracy was last night in meltdown as the entire population took to the streets to protest against themselves.

Anarchists mingled with bearded priests, teachers joined hands with humble goatherds, all demanding one thing – the right not to work.

Said one typical demonstrator, "We are striking in protest against the government's disgraceful plans to stop paying us money for doing nothing."

Up Shit Greek

Said another full-time protestor, Georgiou Paynotaxis, "Who do they think they are, these Germans and Americans in the IMF, telling us that we have to pay our taxes and get rid of corruption?"

PEOPLES OF EUROPE RISE UP

Said Bogos Geriatrikos, a pensioner who recently retired at the age of 46 on double pay, "It is 1940 all over again. We sent the Germans packing the last time they tried to steal all our money, and now all we are asking for is that they should give us 100 billion euros and keep their noses out of our affairs."

TRADITIONAL ANCIENT GREEK PROVERBS

Red sky at night,
Athens alight,
Red sky in the morning,
Another IMF warning.

The Book of Benjamin

Chapter 94

1. And it came to pass that the people of Gaza were sore afflicted. For they were without bread to eat or fish to catch. And even their very houses had been laid waste by the children of Israel.

2. And their cries were heard in many lands, even unto the land of the Turk-ites.

3. Who were meant to be friends of the children of Israel.

4. And the peoples of the earth said one to another, "Let us build a great ark to provide aid and give succour to the afflicted Arab-ites and Hamas-ites that dwell in the land of Gaza".

5. And they took on the ark all manner of goods, including wheelchairs that were loaded two by two, planks of wood that were four by two, bags of cement two hundred by one hundred cubits and all that was needful to build the city of Gaza anew.

6. And they named the ark Navi Marmara, which is to say "Come and get us".

7. And on the ark were all manner of people speaking in a multitude of diverse tongues. That is to say, Swedonians, Hibernians, Netherlandians, Angles, Saxons and of course the Turkites.

8. And there were even among them some of the children of Israel!

9. And, lo, when the ship drew near unto the coast of Gaza, it was seen by the Israel-ites who sent word even unto their leader Benjamin, son of Netan-yahu.

10. And Benjamin waxed wroth and saith unto himself, "What shall I do with this ark? For verily this is a monster coming from the deep like unto a Leviathan who bringeth death and destruction to the children of Israel.

11. Particularly when the Leviathan clearly contains explosives and weapons hidden in the bags of cement which are supplied by the Syrianites and the Iranians."

12. And Benjamin speedily answereth his own question, "I must do what we always do. Smite, smite and smite again. For is it not written 'Smite is right'?"

13. And so it was that, in the darkness, as the ark drew nigh to the shore, and those aboard her were watching their cement by night, the skies were filled with a heavenly host of armed commandos descending from on high and proclaiming "War on earth, ill will to men".

14. Then the activ-ites rose up on the ark, seizing sticks, knives, forks, spoons and whatever other weapons of non-mass-destruction they could layeth their hands on.

15. And they set upon the commandos of Israel who were obliged to respond with the force that is called appropriate.

16. And many of the activ-ites were slain, and even more were taken into captivity.

17. And all the nations of the world (apart, that is, from the Obam-ites) rose up and cried with one voice, "Woe unto Benjamin and the children of Israel. This time they have goneth too far".

18. And Benjamin laughed them to scorn, saying, "That is what you sayeth every time..."

19. "But you do nothing."

20. And Netanyahu looked on what he had done and saw that it was good.

(Continued for ever)

The End Of The Coalition

IT'S less than a month old and yet already the cracks are beginning to appear. The deep divisions that have separated the two parties are even wider now that they are together. Underneath the veneer of unity and purpose lies a dangerous mass of seething columnists who don't want it to work because then they won't have anything to write about and will begin to appear out of touch and sidelined and (*is this right, Ed?*) which is why there can be no doubt that Lord Tebbit is absolutely right when he says, "I hate David Cameron and the only way forward for the Conservative party is to bring back Mrs Thatcher (*You're fired, Ed, or you would be if I had anyone else left on the paper, Ed.*)

HOW LONG WILL IT LAST?

by Phil Space

IT'S THE question every journalist is asking. Will this piece about the coalition be over before it starts or will it go on and on and on?

The indications so far are positive and it looks like there are plenty of words and no shortage of paragraphs.

Only time will tell and there is always a chance that the piece will falter and run out of... er... er... steam... er...

But this is not inevitable. There is no absolute reason why this piece should not last for a thousand words or even longer.

However it could be that forces behind the scenes conspire to end it all suddenly and with no warning. (*You're fired. Ed.*)

A Doctor Fox Writes

AS A Defence Spokesman I am often asked "What are we doing in Afghanistan?".

The simple answer is, "We aren't here to provide health and education to a backward broken 13th century society."

However when I ask my colleagues for a second opinion I realise that my initial diagnosis is completely wrong and we are indeed in Afghanistan to provide health and education to this promising developing country.

If you are worried about Dr Liam Fox, you are probably right.

© Dr Fox 2010

"Been stuck in the traffic long?"

NINTENDO ENNUI

MILESTONES IN ENGLISH HISTORY No. 94

The Great Reform Bill of 2010

THE clamour for reform of the British political system had been growing for several years. It culminated in the famous general election of 2010 when the Liberal Party under its charismatic leader Earl Clegg was swept into power.

But few had anticipated the revolutionary nature of his reforms which, at a stroke, changed the nature of the democratic system and introduced a new era of progress and liberty.

With one fell stroke, Earl Clegg swept away the hated ID cards which had oppressed the populace even though they had yet to come

into existence.

And there was more to come, in the shape of a dramatic promise to look at "the possibility of setting up a committee to investigate Reform of the House of Lords and an even more dramatic promise to have a referendum about the possible introduction of the AV Voting System into the House of Commons at some point in the near future.

Britain had never seen anything like it and Earl Clegg's Bill made all previous political reforms – universal male suffrage, votes for women etc. – seem piffling by comparison with this *(cont. p.94)*

Biblical Times

Friday May 28 10,000 B.C.

CAIN TO CHALLENGE ABEL

by Our Political Staff **Anthony Eden**

TWO brothers have this week both declared themselves as candidates for God's favour in a development that has shocked the world of early politics.

The brothers are the sons of the respected philosopher Adam and his wife Eve, but are considered very different. Cain the older of the two is a crop framer whereas his younger brother Abel is a shepherd and as such both are offering very different sacrifices to God and very different approaches to sorting out the crisis in biblical agriculture.

Miliband of Brothers

However both insist that the contest will be "a civilised affair" and sibling rivalry will be put aside in the interests of creating the stability necessary for

mankind's progress.

Said Cain, holding a banana from one of his fields, "Look I'm not my brother's keeper! One might have expected Abel as the younger brother to do the decent thing and let me get on with it. But since he has now formally declared his candidacy, I am of course delighted and not at all boiling with wrath and vengeance."

Abel was equally quick to calm fears about the possibility of a brotherly feud.

That's Enough Dave and Ed

"I love Cain" he said. "He's my best friend even though he is a bit weird and lacks people skills. But I owe it to mankind to put an alternative point of view and let God choose. I mean that's what

theocracy is all about."

The boys' mother Eve, has refused to take sides. "they are both good boys" she said "and either one would make a very good winner."

Cain however was keen to have the last word. "I know you are looking for a good story to put in the bible but this contest will be perfectly amicable. One thing is for sure, it is not going to end up with me bashing Abel's brains out with a banana and then beng cursed to wander the earth for ever."

ON OTHER PAGES

✝ David goes into coalition with Goliath. "We can work with the Philistines", says Boy King **1**

✝ Angels grounded due to ash cloud **2**

✝ Eden Flower show opens **94**

From The Message Boards

Members of the online community respond to the major issues of the day...

Britain is friendly and welcoming, say refugees

Here's an idea for a survey: how many BRITONS feel welcome in Britain? I see the "refugees" praised British television – hardly surprising, given it consists of foreigners, Moslems and criminals in various nefarious permutations. The "B"BC sports coverage is a national disgrace. Commentators? No, common traitors. – ***Brown_out***

Hundreds of viewers complained to the BBC about the volume of the "vuvuzelas". So did I – they weren't nearly loud enough to drown out Hansen (Scotch), Lawrenson ("Irish"), Klinsmann (German), Seedorf ("Dutch") and their cosmopolitan comrades. – ***Metric_ Martyr***

Hear, hear. On the Today programme John Naughtie casually referred to "Derry or Londonderry, whichever you prefer". How very considerate. What next? Islamabad or Luton, whichever you prefer? Karachi or Bradford, whichever you prefer? – ***Last_taxpayer_standing_in_ the_LiebCon_socialist_paradise***

they make a special ten pound note for refugie's its worth more than normal one's and they get them from the asian post office's, my mate work's at the royle mint and he showed us one ☺ they look the same as other note's so it dont notice – ***Laters***

say your english and they call you a so calld racist☻now there even blamin the BNP for the oil in america – ***Red_White_and_True***

taxpayer i like you're idea of islamabad to be luton but it dont work for "one letter 4 one day" for charity ☺ ive asked wimbledon to be timbledon and england to be eggland in world cup ☺ no news yet but finger's crust! – ***Binny***

Count me in! I'm sucking extra mints for Murry (!) at Timbledon!! – ***Murray_Maniac***

Great stuff guys! – ***Bogbrush***

"A han-n-nd gun!?"

Russell.

Notes & queries

Why are the Olympic mascots called Wenlock and Mandeville?

(Mrs Ephraim McHackey)

⬤ The Rev. Roger Futtworth is completely wrong in linking Wenlock to the Shropshire town of Wenlock Barkworth where the first triple jump, Hop, Skip and Jump, was first contested across the River Wheen or Wen. This is a 19th Century fabrication. Wenlock is a common English herb which goes freely in hedgerows and has been used for centuries to soothe stings caused by insects. Mandeville is, of course, a reference to the 15th Century poet Sir Roger de Mandeville, best known for his ballad "In Sommer cum the ladies". Quite why these names should be used as Olympic mascots remains a mystery to us all.
Dr P.G. Pritt-Stick.

KEEP CALM AND CAMERON

Ariss

FAKE DUCHESS PULLS OFF ANOTHER STING

by Our Scoop Staff **Phil Suitcase**

A News of the World journalist has become the latest victim of the con artist known simply as "The Phoney Fergie".

Claiming to be a duchess, this fifty-year-old mother of two is notorious for tricking gullible members of the media into giving her large sums of money.

In the past she has lured unsuspecting publishers into giving her huge advances by pretending to be a children's author. More recently she fooled diet gurus WeightWatchers into handing over large cheques in the mistaken belief that she was thin.

Fake Handshake

But this latest scam has shocked even the most hardened Fleet Street *(cont. p 94.)*

GLENDA SLAGG
The Gal Who Makes Your Temperature Soar!?!

■ Fergie?? Ferg-off more like!? She's a Right Royal Rotter and no mistake?!! If anyone can bring down the House of Windsor it's this Dumb, Dumped, Dumpy Duchess!?! Duchess of York?, Duchess of Pork Barrel more like – Geddit?!! If you thought sucking toes was bad now she's sucking up to foreign business men!? For half-a-million pounds she says she can open doors?! And is that all you are going to open Ma'am (Geddit?!?) That's the £500,000 Question!? Take a tip from Auntie Glenda and Ferg–off !? *(You've already done that bit. Ed)*

■ Poor Old Fergie! She's just a single Mum on her uppers trying to do the best for her two little kiddies, Bea and Genie!? No wonder she was tempted by the Shady Sheikh from the land of the tabloids! And let's face it he shamefully conned poor old Fergie into asking him for money!?

Imagine it Mister-Self-Righteous-Press-Man! Here's a desperate Duchess with bills to pay and a milkman banging on the door every Monday asking to be paid?!!!

And for why? Because Her Mean Majesty the Queen won't cough up the cash for her down 'n' out daughter-in-law! Shame on you Miserly Ma'am! The sooner Fergie brings down the House of Windsor the better!! All together now: "Fergie's a Jolly Good Duchess!" (You're fired. Ed)

■ *Here they are – Glenda's Macho May Pole Munchkins*

⬤ **Lord Triesman** You can come round and spill some beans at my place, Triesy!?

⬤ **Ronan Keating** OK you're a sneaky lowdown rat!? That's the way I like 'em!? You can scuttle up my drainpipe anytime!?!

⬤ **Mazher Mahamood** he's the Fake Sheikh who exposed Fergie!?! Mmmm!? I'd love to be *entrapped* by you Sheikhy!

Byeeeeee!!

That Fergie Lunch Menu At Mosimann's In Full

Soup du jour
(red or white)

– ✳ –

Coq au vin
(sans coq)

– ✳ –

Brandy snaps
(no snaps)

"I'll pay £500,000 not to meet Prince Andrew"

ME AND MY SPOON

THIS WEEK

SARAH FERGUSON

Do you have a lot of spoons?

I think Sarah isn't in a good place spoon-wise at the moment and she is coming to terms with the fact that she doesn't have as many spoons as she would like…

Why are you talking in the third person?

Sarah is talking in the third person because she's embarrassed about her behaviour. She's been drinking and she's not doing herself any favours. I feel sorry for her.

Could we return to the subject of spoons?

When I divorced my husband, the Royal Family gave me no spoons at all and I respect the Queen for that but it does mean that as a single mother, with two girls to bring up, I have to ask people to give me spoons so that I can feed them…

Have spoons featured prominently in your life?

Little Sarah lost her spoons along the way and that's why she needs a suitcase full of free spoons from you before she will continue the interview.

Has anything amusing ever happened to you in connection with a spoon?

You're not a journalist are you? Oh my God! What's Sarah done now?

⬤ We would like to point out that the Duchess of York donated all free spoons from this interview to her favourite charity – The Sarah Ferguson Spoon Trust, Los Angeles – "working hard to give me a better future."

NEXT WEEK: *Jenson Button, "Me and My Button"*

DIARY

PRINCE CHARLES

SUNDAY: Sunday is traditionally a "day of rest", and I would agree with those, of all faiths, who believe that such a day is of inestimable value to the never-ending "hurly-burly" of today's fast-moving society.

But "no rest for the wicked" as a delightful old ghillie once assured me! I have a number of letters to write, on behalf of the ordinary, decent people of this country, whose voices are seldom, I fear, "heard".

First, I get someone to bring me a pen that actually "works". Why is it, I wonder, that in this modern age, an age in which "technology" has, I fear, "run riot", it still proves so very difficult (if not impossible!), to have one's fountain pen filled as and when one requires it?!! Surely it cannot be beyond the wit of man to devise a system whereby someone makes a regular "check-up" on the quantity of ink in one's pen – and is then able to refill it without being asked until one is "blue in the face"??!!

My first letter is to the Secretary of State for the Environment. "Is it just me" I ask him, "is there a very real danger that "roads" are being permitted to take over our once "green and pleasant land"? Someone was telling me that there is even now a "motorway" – the so-called "M Twenty-Five" that doesn't even go anywhere, but simply goes round and around in a circle, and comes back to exactly that place from which, many ruinously expensive miles before, it began!!! There surely can be no "rhyme nor reason" to such utter madness!"

MONDAY: For some time, I have been meaning to write to the new Secretary of State for Transport. On my last visit to India, I was struck by how immensely civilised their mode of transport was. Some might call it "old-fashioned" but I prefer to call it timeless.

"Forgive me for saying so" I write to the Secretary, "But our own country is literally "crying out" for more elephants. These affectionate creatures, with their long "trunks" and distinctive "silhouette", lend tremendous colour and, above all, character to both town and country. Surely any halfway-civilised country would be hard-pressed to come up with an argument against riding atop these marvellous animals rather than being squeezed shoulder-to-shoulder with countless hundreds of others within the cramped confines of a "double-decky bus" or "underground tube train"?"

TUESDAY: A brief letter to our new Secretary of State for Health. "I really do not think I am alone in being deeply concerned at the amount of "tomato ketchup" and "chips" being consumed these days. I know that, like me, most patients would infinitely prefer to be given the more traditional and, above all, life-enhancing option of our ever-popular low-salt rosemary and thyme organic wheaten oat-cakes."

WEDNESDAY: I hear back from the new Prime Minister of Australia. She's evidently delighted by my few kind words of advice, as these people so often are. She adds that though her government has no plans, in the immediate future, for demolishing the modernist eyesore that is the "Sydney Opera House" and changing it for something better-suited to the surrounding "environment", she will certainly bear in mind my suggestion for a more classically-proportioned and "in keeping" Regency-style opera house. Hugely encouraging news: copies to our new Prime Minister, the Presidents of France, Italy, Germany, Canada and the USA, the Dalai Lama, Quinlan Terry and 52 others.

THURSDAY: Plough my way through a backlog of letters The first is to the Chairman of "Tesco", suggesting that to replace his "fleet" of "lorries", etc, for the good old-fashioned horse-and-cart would represent a tremendous saving on fossil fuel, as well as being infinitely better for the environment and perhaps he would care to drop round to Clarence House to discuss it? It's so often the "personal touch" that swings these people round to a more enlightened point of view.

I then write a sensitive letter to "The Director-General of the BBC" (what very grand titles these people like to give themselves!!). "Forgive me for writing" I begin, "But I only do so out of a particular concern for the future of broadcasting in this country". I then make a tentative suggestion for more "peak time" programmes – perhaps one or two of them a day – devoted to the age-old benefits of homeopathic medicine.

I add, "Believe me, I am not alone in being continually surprised by how very few homeopathic doctors appear on a regular basis in a popular series such as "Casualty".

FRIDAY: Judging from his response, The Secretary of State for Health is tremendously excited by my proposals for a more wheaten-oatcake-based outlook in our NHS. I pride myself on recognising the tell-tale signs of official enthusiasm: on a copy of my original letter comes his shorthand code for "Brilliant – Interesting – Neighbourly", or "BIN" for short. Not everything, I fear, is perfect in our hidebound world, but we are "making strides". It all goes to show that there's nothing quite so effective, in these increasingly "hectic" days, as a hand-written letter.

As told to CRAIG BROWN

WORLD'S LARGEST CHIP PAN

HUGE GULF OF MEXICO DISCOVERY

BP last night was hailing the discovery of the world's largest chip pan in the Gulf of Mexico.

"If initial estimates of its size pan out, it could be producing hundreds of thousands of barrels of Freedom Fries a day.

"This could make the US self-sufficient in Happy Meals until last weekend."

BP BOSS REASSURES WORLD

I'm here to pour oil on troubled waters

"Then, like you, I began to feel the C of E had lost its way..."

Saville Report on Peterloo Massacre Published After 190 Years

BY OUR HISTORY STAFF TRISTRAM HUNT

LORD SAVILLE, 181, has strongly criticised the conduct of the British Army during a peaceful protest in St Peter's Field, near Manchester, which led to the "unnecessary deaths" of a number of innocent civilians.

In a shock report, Saville found that the soldiers "lost control" and used their sabres indiscriminately on the unarmed demonstrators.

In particular the judge singled out the actions of Dragoon F, who was responsible for cutting down no fewer than fifteen of the marchers but then claimed in evidence to the Saville inquiry that he had been at Ascot at the time.

Saville Row

The commanding officer of the 15/16 Hussars, Col. Cholmondley Warburton-Smythe, was also criticised for telling his men to "have a good crack at these Lefties". No sooner was the report published than a galaxy of eminent historians, led by Sir Andrew Roberts, paid tribute to Lord Saville for "at last unearthing the truth about that fateful August day in 1819".

"Up to this time," said Sir Andrew, "we had all assumed that the Hussars had acted in self-defence, after they had been attacked by a rabble of murderous Fenians and Jacobins, led by Orator Hunt and Martin McGuinness."

Bloody Sunday Times

Yesterday the Prime Minister, David Cameron, apologised to the people of Manchester for a "grave wrong" for which he personally had been in no way responsible.

Asked if there would be any prosecutions of the soldiers responsible for the massacre, Mr Cameron said that this would be a matter for the legal authorities, though he understood that the fact that they were all dead might present some "technical problems".

He ended by saying that he would continue to support British soldiers wherever they were and whatever they were doing and that he was proud to be British."

On Other Pages

■ *"I Was There"* by Sir Max Hastings ■ *"So Was I"* by Simon Winchester ■ *"I Wasn't But It Won't Stop Me Writing About It"* by Everyone Else
Plus ● Was Orator Hunt carrying a sawn-off blunderbuss? Special 94-page investigation.

SAVILLE REPORT
PM's Non-Apology in Full

IN A startlingly frank statement to a hushed House of Commons, the Prime Minister David Cameron yesterday failed to apologise for giving £200 million of public money to the lawyers involved in the Saville Inquiry.

Bloody Pay Day

"Let's be frank," he said, "the lawyers acted wrongly. Spinning this out for 12 years was totally unjustifiable and this is a shameful day for the entire legal profession."

"I still, however, maintain," continued Mr Cameron, "that our British lawyers are the best in the world."

Said one reporter, Sir Simon Winchester, "When the army of British lawyers first moved into Northern Ireland 12 years ago, they were welcomed by the local population.

Para Legals

But as the years dragged by and the losses to the taxpayer continued to mount, resentment grew and the lawyers were subjected to almost incessant attacks on them from the *Daily Mail*."

The lawyers are, however, unrepentant. Said one yesterday, "If you accuse us of being no more than greedy, money-grabbing parasites we'll sue you for every penny you've got."

● On other pages: Bloody Sunday – was BP to blame? asks US Congress

---

POETRY CORNER

**In Memoriam
Egon Ronay, food critic
and restaurateur**

So. Farewell
Then
Egon Ronay.

Food critic and
Restaurateur.

"Egon Toast",
That was one of the jokes
Keith and I
Used to make about you.

"Egon Face",
That was another.

And now we say
"Egon to a better place".

E. Gon Thribb (17½)

Restaurant Review

The Upstairs

Bland, cloud-themed decor, waiters wearing ridiculous "winged" outfits. Incessant harp music soon gets on nerves. Food unspeakable – had to send the ambrosia back and the nectar was corked. Service appalling – you might have to wait 1,000 years. Frankly, I wouldn't be seen dead in a place like this.

Egon Ronay

COMING SOON

New version of the classic story in which Ridley Scott takes money from the poor cinema-goer and gives it to the rich, ie himself and Russell Crowe.

A brilliant depiction of the Middle Aged *(surely "Ages"? Ed.)* as Robin Hood (Russell Crowe) piles on the pounds *(surely "drama"? Ed.)*. Will Cate Blanchett's reputation survive? Will the peasants rebel and go and see Iron Man 2 instead? *(No, because that is **really** boring. Ed.)*

"When I grow up I want to be undead"

Exclusive to

PRIVATE EYE

GENUINE PHOTOS OF PIERS MORGAN'S WEDDING

THESE amazing photos, given to Private Eye by a 100% reputable source, show Piers Morgan and his lovely bride on their special day.

These pictures are not at all fakes and have been thoroughly checked and authenticated by the editor himself.

Here comes the Moron

You may now kiss the Moron

Do you take this Moron?

Mr & Mrs Moron

BUDGET CUT SHOCK

THE Coalition Government said the first phase of the consultation into cuts has revealed that people want the services used by other people cut.

"We found that 100% of people wanted the services they used regularly to be retained," said a Treasury spokesman, "but the flipside of that was that 100% of people were very keen to see services they didn't use slashed to the bone.

"It's clear that as long as we only cut services used by other people, the public will be fully behind our austerity programme."

TV Highlights

'IS FROST DEAD?' – asks Satire

BBC4 Monday 9.00 pm

BACK in the 1960's it seemed as if David Frost was changing the world, making presidents and dictators listen. But now he has no effect on anything much.

In this probing documentary David Frost falls asleep as he speaks to some of satire's most famous names to pose the vital question –

Is DAVID FROST DEAD?

★ **Eye Rating** – That Was Weak, That Was.

"Those in favour say 'uh-uh'"

TURDS BACK AT NUMBER ONE

by Our Rock 'n' Roll Staff
Professor Norman Stone

Forty years after it was first released the Turds' seminal album "Tax Exile On Turd Street" has been re-released and has become the best-selling CD this week.

In "Turd Street", as it has become known, Spiggy and the Band unashamedly celebrate the hedonistic summer of 1971 – the booze, the pills, the girls, the punch-ups – they're all there in the greatest act of rock 'n' roll rebellion ever to be recorded.

Said leader of the Turds, Sir Spiggy Topes, 84, "Frankly old boy, it has come as something of a shock. I can't even remember recording it in the first place. Are you sure it is one of ours?"

He continued, "You must excuse me, I have to go to Lords because England are playing Bangladesh and it doesn't do to turn up late and miss the toss of the coin, especially in a wheel chair, well toodle-pip, must dash."

BP TO PLUG LEAK WITH BLUE WHALE

by Our Environmental Staff **Louise Iana**

"WE'RE hoping we can get a Blue Whale to swim into the area and then into the cracked pipeline which now has a really huge hole in it." said a BP spokesperson. "Our experts think it will become wedged and stop the flow of oil, though of course some may come out of its spout. We are looking for a suitable Blue Whale and the plan is to lure it to the site by trailing BBQ flavoured plankton in front of it.

Asteroid

If the Blue Whale doesn't work we are considering trying to get an asteroid to smash into The Gulf of Mexico. It has been done before we think, and might plug the leak, though it might mean it destroys life on Earth as we know it but that would be a small price to pay. There are loads of asteroids about…I'm sure we could get one and push it towards Earth with the Space Station.

Lizard People

If that fails we could probably come in from below the pipeline by travelling through the centre of the Earth, going in under the Polar Ice Cap. We could talk to the Lizard People who live there and arrange for transportation through the molten core in special heat resistant suits and come up and plug the leak by spraying boiling lava into the pipeline, although this might have adverse effects on the soft-shell crabs. *(cont. p. 94)*

(cont. p. 94)

"The baddies are always English"

OIL SPILL BREAKTHROUGH

by Our Media Staff **Rowan Pellican**

AT LAST. After weeks of nail-biting tension, the teams working round the clock on the BP oil spillage have claimed a breakthrough.

Yes, viewers all over the world were finally shown the image that they had hoped and prayed for – a bird covered in oil.

Said one tired but delighted media worker, Phil Space, "I can't tell you how happy we all are here. This picture of the bird means that at long last I can write the words, 'This Tragic Symbol of the Environmental Catastrophe That Has Shaken the World'."

He continued, "After nearly a

month of agonised waiting, I am home and dry. Which is more than I can say about the pelican."

● **More pictures of bird covered in oil, 2-35.**

The Disillusion Honours List

Life Peerages to:

John Prescott, for services to amateur croquet and his secretary.

Beverley Hughes, for services to covering up the truth in the field of immigration.

Quentin Davies, for services to the turncoat industry in jumping ship from the Conservative Party.

Dr John Reid, for his services in winning the war in Afghanistan without a shot being fired.

Dr Paul Boateng, for services to bullying black members of staff while on secondment in Capetown.

Ms Sue Nye, for services to being bullied by the former prime minister while working at 10 Downing Street.

John Gummer, for services to the beefburger sector and

One lard a-leaping

for his contribution to the destruction of the British fishing industry.

Michael Howard, for services to the Transylvanian community and the Involuntary Blood Transfusion Authority.

Ian Paisley, for services to the Roman Catholic Church.

(That's enough Dissolute Honours, Ed.)

TOP POLICEMAN GIVEN PEERAGE – DID THEY GET THE WRONG MAN?

by Our Crime Staff **Eddie Aim-Fire**

IN WHAT could be a tragic case of mistaken identity, the former Metropolitan Police Commander, Sir Ian Blair, has been targeted to become a Member of the House of Lords.

Said one expert, "They were looking for a distinguished senior policeman to serve in the Upper House but due to a terrible muddle they have chosen the man who oversaw the Menezes shooting."

As calls grew for an inquiry into the Lord Blair affair, insiders are blaming a lack of communication between the Palace and Scotland Yard.

Lock, Stock and Two Smoking Barrels

Said one, "Sir Ian looked a bit like the man we were looking for but if the authorities had kept in touch, perhaps by watching the news, they would have known that Sir Ian Blair was an entirely innocent man."

"He was just in the right place at the right time and sadly he ended up dead lucky."

Summer Menu with Mike Rowave

The Eye's TV celebrity chef gets set for the hot weather

Ingredients	Recipe	Comments
Tomato	1. Buy tomato 2. Eat it.	Mmm!

© M. Rowave

'MY SECRET SHAME' by David Laws

by Lib E. Perves

FOR YEARS, Treasury Minister David Laws lived with a secret that even his closest friends knew nothing about.

But now the Lib Dem Laws admits, "I am a practising Conservative."

SHOCK HORROR

"Don't forget," he told me, "there was a time not so long ago when if a Lib Dem fancied cutting taxes or putting people on the dole that was considered criminal. But nowadays, with the coalition and so forth ,it's become perfectly acceptable.

"And in those days you worried about what your parents would think if you came to them and confessed, 'Dad, I'm a Tory but I can't help it *(cont. p. 94)*

We've agreed to a fixed grin parliament

HE'S DEAD SO I'LL PRESCRIBE HIM SOME TABLETS FOR THAT

colin Wheeler

Should the Red Ken be reintroduced into London?

by Our Nature Staff **Michael Kite**

THE Red Ken, so rare that only one of it is thought to exist, may be reintroduced into London.

The Red Ken became extinct in 2008 and many Londoners missed its distinctive nasal whining cry. The Red Ken loved newts but waged war on pigeons, ruthlessly eliminating them from Trafalgar Square.

Said one Londoner, "We've had enough of this old scavenger. He's been shitting on us from a great height for years."

Others welcomed the idea of the Red Ken's return. Dave Spart, 45, a student, said, "Er... basically it's time to eradicate totally and utterly the Blue Boris which to my mind is frankly, er..."

● **See more pix of the Red Ken having a drink and pushing someone off a wall.**

BP'S NEW PLAN TO STAUNCH FLOW

by Our Engineering Staff **Phil Gulf**

BP have come up with an ingenious new solution to their problems in the Gulf of Mexico, which involves lowering an enormous bucket over President Obama's head.

The bucket, weighing over half a ton and made out of reinforced, sound-proof concrete, is designed to stop the outpouring of criticism of BP from the American President.

Nicknamed "Operation Shut-thefuckup", BP engineers hope that at long last they can stop the President gushing.

"We've got a lot riding on this," said BP Chief Executive Tony Haywire, "and with any luck, we will contain all the Obama inside the bucket. Then we will be free once again to carry on our business of fouling the world." *(Surely "fuelling"? Ed.)*

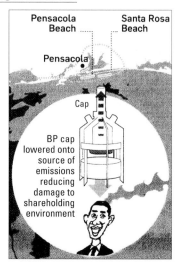

Pensacola Beach — Santa Rosa Beach

Pensacola

Cap

BP cap lowered onto source of emissions reducing damage to shareholding environment

On other pages

● Should Haywire be shot by firing squad or executed by more humane lethal injections? ask US protestors, **94**

ANTIQUES ROAD SHOW

Man with bow tie and silly voice: Now this is a very interesting item. It's a bum, probably early 21st Century, very well preserved.

We can see that it's been given a denim cover and it seems to have won some sort of prize... *"Rear of the Year 2010"* I think. Let me just put my spectacles on...

Yes, that's right... this is a very exciting arsefact...

now, where did you get this, did you say? I think this bum could be very valuable. I hope you have got it insured because if it came up at auction, I think it would fetch a very substantial bum... sorry, sum... silly me... I don't suppose that you are going to part with it though, are you?

Fiona Bruce *(for it is her bum)*: And the latest news from Afghanistan where three *(cont. Channel 94)*

Real Seaworld

-PILBROW-

POETRY CORNER

In Memoriam
Walter Frederick
Morrison

So. Farewell
Then
Walter Frederick Morrison
Inventor
Of the Frisbee.

Sadly
Unlike your
Invention

You won't
Be coming
Back.

      E.J. Thribbee (17½)

In Memoriam
Dick Francis

Also. Farewell
Then
Dick Francis
Jockey and
Thriller writer.

You died aged
89.

Yes, you had a
Good run.

      E.J. Thribb (17½-1)

In Memoriam
The Reader's Digest

So. Farewell
Then Reader's
Digest.
Once the best read
Magazine in the
World.

You were famous for
Such features as
*Laughter is the best
Medicine.*

So let's all have
A good
Laugh.

      E.J. Thribb (17½)

● *A Reader's Digest abridged
version of this poem is
available below:*

*So. Farewell.
Ha, ha, ha.*

*(Adapted from the original by
Russell Twisk)*

FIRST DRAFTS

Sausage on the brain again, Oscar...

Oscar Wilde

An author has a lucrative deal with a publisher to keep delivering dilemma novels – but they are getting increasingly ridiculous – Does she deliver them anyway?

Jodi Picoult

Dear sir,
Re your overdraft,
Weialala leia
Jug jug jug jug jug
Chantant dans la couple!
Tereu.
And let that be an end
to the matter
Yours etc...

The letters of T.S. Eliot

Hmmn... no delete key...

Dan Brown "The Lost Symbol"

In Memoriam
Peter Graves,
Mr Phelps in TV's
Mission Impossible

So. Farewell
Then.
Peter Graves,
TV's Mr Phelps.

"Your mission,
Jim, should you
Choose to accept
It…"

Yes,
That was the programme's
Catchphrase.

"This tape will
Self-destruct in 10
Seconds."
That was another.

Now you have
Gone on your
Final mission.

The one where
We all
Self-destruct.

All together now
Da Da Da
Dum Dum Dum
Diddle Dee. Diddle Dee
Etc.

      E.J. Thribb (17½)

In Memoriam
Eugene Terreblanche,
South African
Politician

So. Farewell

Then.
Eugene Terreblanche,
Racist and lunatic.

You have been murdered.

A sad end
To a long
And undistinguished
Career.

However one
Question strikes
Me.

Will everyone at
Your funeral
Have to wear
White?

      E.J. Thribb (17½)
      Oxford Professor of
      Poetry Designate.

FINAL WORLD CUP SQUAD REVEALED

By Our New Football Correspondent **Toke N. Celebrity**

THERE was some surprise today as "sick as a parrot" was left out of the final twenty-four clichés being taken by the England commentators to the World Cup.

"Sick as a parrot" has performed well at this level in the past, but he just didn't impress when brought on as a cliché in the second half of England's friendly with Japan.

"Obviously this is a game of two halves," said Alan Hanson, "but at the end of the day you've got to feel sorry for the cliché that's left out."

"I was surprised, as for a big cliché he was always surprisingly light on his feet," added Gary Lineker, "but this just goes to show you that football is a funny old game."

Vuvuzelas, thousands of them

ENGLAND TEAM CONFRONTED BY NUTTER –

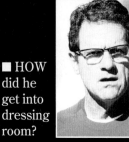

■ HOW did he get into dressing room?

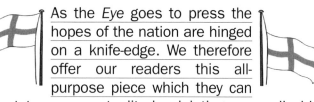

As the *Eye* goes to press the hopes of the nation are hinged on a knife-edge. We therefore offer our readers this all-purpose piece which they can adapt to any eventuality by deleting as applicable

There was only one word for England's performance last night. Shameful/Brilliant. Fabio Cappello should hold his head in shame/be given a knighthood following this defeat/victory/draw. Rooney was world class/sent off and Gerrard led by example/should be shot.

No wonder the thousands of fans in South Africa booed/cheered as England crashed out/sailed through to the next round.

They think it's all over – it is now/it isn't yet.

© *All newspapers*

Notes&queries

Where does the word 'Vuvuzela' come from?

(Mrs Ludmilla Rubenstein)

● The curious name of this primitive African instrument owes its origins to a remark made by the French composer Claude Debussy when travelling with his great friend, the Comtesse Silvestri. In a Cape Town music shop, Debussy's eye was caught by a strange trumpet-like instrument and he remarked to his companion "Avez-vous vu cela?" ("Have you seeen this"?). Ravel later included the vuvuzela in one of his orchestral compositions, "Le Mort de Babar".

Ethel Barenboim.

● Mrs Barenboim is sadly mistaken betraying a typically euro centric view of African history. The vuvuzela, for her information, is a traditional war trumpet originally made from the horn of the water buffalo or "vuvu" in the local Zela tongue. There is a reference in Baden-Powell's classic account of the Vuvu wars, *Through Bush and Veldt (1883)*; "You can hear the Zelas playing their vuvus from dawn to dusk and a pretty terrifying sound it is. I can see England losing this war and having to go home early."

Professor Aaron G. String, University of Ruislip (formerly Tyre Planet).

● Sadly the explanation behind the ubiquitous vuvuzela is rather more prosaic than your correspondents have so far suggested. The instrument is of modern origin and is made in China in the industrial province of Zhu Zhu from a composite polyresin known as zelane (CH_4OOCH_4-OOHC). Unsurprisingly when exported to South Africa by the VanderBastard corporation of Johannesburg the plastic trumpets became known to the locals as "vuvuzelas".

Simon Google-Smith.

Answers please to the following:
Were there ever gladiatorial contests in Milton Keynes? How do you count the number of whales left in the sea? Why have we heard so little recently of the actor James Corden?

WORLD CUTS
GREECE | UK
PORTUGAL
ETC

Grizelda

BP PORTRAIT COMPETITION WINNER ANNOUNCED

Pelican 2010, Oil on water, measuring 20,000 square miles.
Price $20 trillion

Daily Cairograph

Friday, 9th July, 2589 BC

Prince Interfered in Landmark Building Development

BY OUR ANCIENT HISTORY STAFF **NILE FERGUSSON**

ARCHITECTS are furious with the Prince of Egypt for what they describe as "meddling" in the design of the prestigious Royal Tomb Complex at Giza.

Said one architect, "This is a Grade One site in the centre of the capital and it was a chance to create a lasting architectural statement. Yet the Pharaoh has yet again shoved his oar in and demanded a boring traditional design."

In a papyrus to the Middle-Eastern developer, Prince Cheops wrote, "I am reluctant to get involved, but if you don't do what I want, I'll have you eaten alive by scarab beetles and then burnt in boiling oil."

Observers say that reading between the lines this sends out a clear message that Prince Cheops wants things his way – and we are going to be stuck for eternity with these unoriginal, dull, pastiche, fuddy-duddy pyramid structures rather than something modern and exciting in steel and glass – whatever they are.

SAATCHI DONATES RUBBISH COLLECTION TO NATION

by Our Arts Staff **Brian R. Sewell**

THE reclusive billionaire philanthropist Mr Charles Saatchi last night announced that he was giving his entire rubbish collection to the nation.

The move has been hailed as the most generous gesture ever made by a patron of the arts. The collection is currently housed in a wheelie bin outside Mr Saatchi's Eaton Place mansion and includes a number of iconic pieces including:

● **Kentucky Fried Chicken Bucket (family size)**
● **Tesco's own brand bleach bottle (dented)**
● **60 egg shells (loose)**
● **Tub of Waitrose Taramasalata (unopened, past sell-by date,**

4th May 2008)
● **One pickled herring**
● **Rusty potato peeler (with peel)**
● **Contents of hoover bag**
● **One Ibuprofen tablet (still in packet)**

The Arts Minister, Daryl Easel (Lib Dem, Emin East) thanked M. Saatchi for his astonishing generosity. "These are the most important items of British rubbish of the last century. Not only has Mr Saatchi allowed us to take his wheelie bin away for free, he has donated a big hole in the ground in which the rubbish can be tipped and viewed by members of the public in perpetuity."

"No! No! No! Your skirt needs to be much shorter"

MASTERCLASS

by Our Cuts Staff **Jeremy Axeman**

THERE was widespread public disbelief yesterday when the government announced that its programme of cuts would involve things being cut.

Said one amazed voter, "This isn't what we voted for. When they all said there would have to be cuts we had no idea that they meant actually cutting things."

Public service chiefs were equally aghast: "I mean we all accept the need for cuts to sort out the economy, but cutting jobs, pensions, money, funding, investment programmes and that sort of thing well that's going too far."

He continued, 'We want cuts that don't involve any cuts. That's not too much to ask is it?"

PLUS ● "If you cut my budget then millions of people will die horribly," says everyone facing cuts **2** ● UK to sell off islands in order to raise money. Wight, Man, Sheppey, Conway, Dogs, Northern, all to go **94**

SOON NOT TO BE A NEW HOSPITAL AFTER ALL

BANX

Exclusive to all newspapers

TOP RUSSIAN SPY REVEALED AS FRUITY

by Our Espionage Staff **Adrian Mole**

A TOP Russian spy working in America has sensationally been exposed as "very fruity indeed".

The undercover Soviet agent, who for years has been stealing American secrets and passing information to her Russian bosses, was last week discovered to be a pouting red-headed lovely of the type you could put on the front page of the Telegraph.

From Russia with Lovely

Said a top CIA spymaster, "We knew for years that she was involved with espionage, but had no idea that she was leading a double life as a gorgeous flame-haired temptress."

Newspapers all over the world were stunned by the revelation. Said one top editor, "This begs the important question. How many more fruity spies are there out there still at large? And can we put them on the front page of our papers to liven up the news?"

On other pages

THE Sun

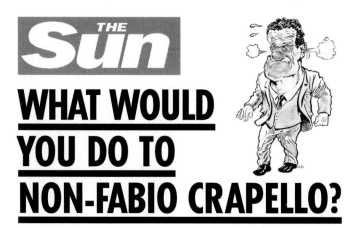

WHAT WOULD YOU DO TO NON-FABIO CRAPELLO?

YOU decide on the fate of the worst England manager since the last one

1. Sack him and don't pay him a penny.
2. Forcibly deport him to Italy with a hood over his head.
3. String him up just like they did to Mussolini.
4. Burn him at the stake like they did to Joan of Arc when we beat the French.
5. Hang, draw and quarter him and feed his entrails to the ravens like they did in the days when they knew how to deal with traitors.
6. Brand the word "paedophile" on his forehead and curse him to wander the globe forever. *(That's enough incitement to murder, Ed.)*

Who should be the new England manager?

You decide on the best candidate to fill soccer's no.1 hotseat

1. David Beckham
2. Theo Paphitis of Dragon's Den
3. Sir Stephen Fry
4. Boris Johnson
5. Jamie Oliver
6. Joanna Lumley
7. Pele
8. Vince Cable
9. Diane Abbott
10. Sir Peregrine Worsthorne

WHY ARE ENGLAND PLAYERS 'STILL BREATHING'? asks the Sun

England's pampered multi-millionaire World Cup failures showed their utter contempt for the fans today after they were pictured just hours after the match breathing openly with no shame at all.

"I've paid good money to be here," said one angry England supporter in a curly wig, "and there they are, breathing and sitting on chairs and standing up and wearing clothes. It's a disgrace."

"I'm really glad Margaret Thatcher isn't alive today to see this lack of respect and utter contempt for the English flag which I've got painted on my buttocks."

ON OTHER PAGES: ● Don't Blame Capello says the Sun

ENGLAND SUPPORTERS HEAD FOR MARS

England supporters today set out for Mars for the 2130 World Cup, confident that the team can end 170 years of World Cup misery.

"Despite our losses to Guernsey and The Falklands in the qualifying rounds, we're sure we can do it," said one fan, wearing antennae and a "Fuck off Martians" t-shirt.

"Granted, our friendly loss to the Galapagos Islands was a disappointment, but that tortoise did a great header into the goal. It's the long necks, innit? That's evolution for you.

"All we've got to do is beat Germany for the first time since 1966, how hard can that be?

"The last time was a disaster, and it was all the fault of that rubbish alien manager we had, Flabbilon Kapellax from Alpha Centauri. Why we put our trust in an alien I don't know. England shoud always have a human manager. The tentacles unnerve our boys."

The hologram of Sir Alf Ramsay, who took over managing the side after 2126, said his first move would be for the players to wear long shorts and eat pork pies at half-time.

Before   **After**

ADVERTISEMENT

---

the WORLD C***S

PAUL WOOD

FABIO, JUST A FEW WEEKS AGO YOU SAID ENGLAND COULD WIN THE WORLD CUP

PRESS

YES...

...2014!

BLOODY GENIUS

I DIDN'T SEE THAT COMING

HE MIGHT BE ONTO SOMETHING

...AND SO IT BEGINS AGAIN...

LIB DEM RUNS OFF WITH 'WOMAN'

by Our Political Staff **Lembit Ontheside**

IT EMERGED yesterday that a senior Liberal Democrat MP, Chris Huhe, has left his wife for a woman – who turns out not to be a man.

An opposition spokesman said, "Yet again, we see the Lib Dems betraying their principles in a vain attempt to impress the Tories.

The Lib Dem leader Nick Cleggover, however, said, "To be fair to Chris, he has run off with a woman who has short spiky hair and used to live with another woman so it's not as bad as (*cont. p. 94*)

"Bad news mein Führer, the octopus says we lose Stalingrad"

Notes & queries

Why did Liberal Democrat MP Mr Huhne's new partner Carina Trimingham object to journalists saying she wore 'Doc Marten' boots?

(Rev. Vernon Schwarzenegger)

● The association of lesbianism with these famous items of footwear has passed into common parlance – hence the resolutely bisexual Ms Trimingham's reluctance to be stereotyped. This thinking dates back to the song "These Doc Marten boots are made for walking up Old Compton Street", most famously recorded by the late Dusty Springfield in 1963.

Mrs Bertie Burlington.

● Mrs Burlington is sorely mistaken. The Doc Marten boot has been a favourite among gardeners since the 1930s, and was particularly popularised by Ursula Trubshawe, a close friend of Vita Sackville-West, the doyenne of lesbian gardeners.

I have a photograph of her in the legendary "Pink Garden" at Sissinghurst, wearing her Doc Martens and little else!

Rosamund Russell-Twisk.

● Miss Russell-Twisk's fanciful attempt to unravel the Doc Marten/Sapphic conundrum is at least 500 years out of date. As all art historians know only too well, the boot owes its name to the 16th century Flemish painter Dirk Maartens (1525-1591?). Maartens specialisd in genre paintings of peasant life, often showing women toiling in the fields, wearing sturdy laced-up leather boots. These boots became known, after the painter, as "Dirk Maartens", later corrupted to "Doc Martens". There is no connection of any kind with lesbianism or Old Compton Street.

Prof. Denis von Bulow.

Answers please to the following:
Which country has, per capita, the most postmen? Is it true that the Babylonians invented the coat hanger? Why is custard yellow?

WORLD CUP FINAL
OUTBREAK OF FOOTBALL RUINS EXHIBITION OF VIOLENCE

by Our Soccer Staff **Trevor Booking**

IT WAS meant to be a world class display of thuggery and aggression but lovers of the "ugly game" were disappointed by flashes of football which marred an otherwise unpleasant spectacle.

Said a disappointed Dutch fan Sid Bjonkers, "I was gutted for sure. I came to see 90 minutes of hacking, shirt-grabbing and diving. Instead there were moments of passing, dribbling and even at one point a goal, would you believe?"

His wife, Doris Bjonkers agreed, "I did not travel all this way to see Iniesta, how you say, hitting the back of the net with clinical precision. No, I am blaming the referee for gaining control of the match and sending off one of our players."

One of the BBC's match commentators, Gary Vinegar, was forced to agree, "If people want to watch football then that's fine but it's not what the World Cup is all about."

Luckily most experts felt that the final was not typical of the entire tournament. Said ITV's James Corden, "There were enough incidences of cynical fouls, professional handballs and outrageous play acting to remind fans that the tournament is still the greatest advertisement for lack of sportsmanship at its very (*cont. 2094.*)

AFGHANISTAN
Exit Timetable Announced

by Our Military Staff **Phil Graves**

THE announcement of a withdrawal of British soldiers from the conflict in Afghanistan has provoked immediate controversy. Said one senior military officer, "Setting the date as 'Never' is far too early and puts too much pressure on our chaps in the field."

Another General agreed. "'Never' is just being unrealistic given the progress we have made to date. I fear that never is too soon and it might take twice as long as that to effect real change."

Mayor of London in New Bonking Crisis

Cripes! Not likely! What makes you think that? What a load of piffle!

IS BORIS THE FATHER?

The Hon EMMA SOAMES Grand-daughter of Sir Winston Churchill writes exclusively for the Eye about the Boris Johnson Affair

Why are all these horrid common people going on about dear old Boris and his baby? Those of us who actually belong to the upper classes know that this is how we do things – everyone jumping into bed with everyone else and having a jolly good laugh about it. No one is vulgar enough to make a fuss or have a divorce just because hubby has got someone else preggers! Really, how infradig darling. © G. Soames 2010

IT'S MUMMY, DARLING, I'M PICKING YOU UP AT THE END OF TERM – I HAVE FAIR HAIR AND I'LL BE WEARING A GREEN COAT

GLENDA SLAGG
She's getting hotter all the time

■ BORIS!?!! What a disgrace!? Getting his leg over someone else's posh totty and leaving her up the duff!! He's meant to be running London – but he can't even keep his trousers up!! So there's another bastard running around – and I don't mean Boris stoopid?!? Come on Mrs so-called Johnson and get your rolling pin out. It's time to give BoJo the Heave Ho and tell him to jump on his bike and peddle off into the sunset!?!!

■ BORIS!?! What's all the fuss about, Mr Prude??! So Bonking Boris has got his leg over someone else's posh totty and left her up the duff!!? So what??! That's what we voted for – a bit of rumpy pumpy fun in po-faced politics!?! Good on BoJo and his Mojo!! You put a smile on our faces and if Mrs Johnson doesn't like it, my advice sweetheart is jump on your old man's bike and peddle off into the sunset!!?

■ SELINA SCOTT!?! Arenchasick-ofher!? A-whingein' and a-whinin', a-moanin' and a-groanin' about ageism at Aunty Beeb!!? OK, so they keep givin' jobs to fruity young babes to get the fellas a-dribblin' and a-droolin' as they hear that two more soldiers have been killed in Afghanistan (You're fired, Ed.) So how do you think *you* got a job a hundred years ago, Grandma??!! It wasn't for the size of your brain, dear!?? Why don't you just put a sock in it, you old bag (no offence) and take a zimmer frame for a walk down the day-care centre??!!

■ HATS OFF to Selina Scott!?! At last someone's got the guts to stand up to the totty-obsessed tyrants at the BBC!?! Face facts, Mister News Boss, with age comes wisdom and no-one's wiser than Selina, she's got it in spades!!? Let's get her and all the other grand dames of yesteryear to tell us two more soldiers have been killed in Afghanistan (You're fired, Ed.)

■ HERE THEY ARE – Glenda's Barbecue Beefcakes?!?!

● **Howard Webb!?!!** Britain's toughest ref – I'm a naughty girl so come round and give me one of your cards (Geddit??!!)

● **Dr Liam Fox!?!!** How would you like to creep into my bedroom and give me a bite, Foxy??!!

● **Lewis Oosthuizen!?!!** Crazy name, crazy golfer!?!!

Byeee!!

...Here in South Korea, it is beyond us why people continue endlessly to send in letters, signing them with what are clearly made-up names.

Y. KI PON.

...Please do not stop this wonderful column. We are sailing to China and in the long hours we entertain ourselves by re-reading your lovely magazine and especially Pseudo Names. Do continue.

HONOR SLOH-BOHT.

...As a Frenchman recently made redundant, I find myself with time to indulge in pointless past-times.

GUY ZAJOB.

...As French lavatory attendants, we've been entertained by a spate of graffiti on the walls of our esteemed establishment here in Paris. We've a suspicion that it is inspired by your esteemed magazine.

B DAY, P SOIR.

...Unlike my compatriots B. Day and P. Soir, I find Pseudo Names pretty ordinary fare.

VANDA TABLE.

...The way in which the EU appointed its President shows that they've gone mad.

TOULOUSE LE PLOT.

... If you ever decide to form a First XI of made-up names, you will need a coach. I wish to put my name forward for this position. I am an internationally renowned coach. I am particularly good with the pictures I use in team talks.

SVEN DIAGRAM.

...It is said that no man is an island. I disagree.

BARRY (Wales).

...I have at last succeeded in obtaining a copy of your esteemed organ here in Thailand.

TUK SUM GETTIN.

... The diverse peoples of the former Soviet Union are really appreciating your Pseudo Names feature. Keep it going or the gas gets turned off.

BELLA ROOSE,
GEORGIA AND MOLL DOVER
U. CRANE, R. MEANYER.

...I hope Scottish contributions to the Pseudo Names feature are valued as much as those from south of the border and that there is no mechanism preventing our northern neighbours from taking part in the debate?

ADRIAN SWALL.

...Not all former Russian states are enamoured with Pseudo Names. There's no way that such nonsense would be tolerated here in Uzbekistan.

SAM R. KAND.

...I must take issue with your previous correspondent, for it is widely known that a strong Pseudo Names underground movement exists in Uzbekistan and other former Soviet republics.

TASH (KENT).

...Of course, it is internationally recognised that German Pseudo Names are the best.

DOT SCHLAND
HUGH BERRALLES.

...Re: "German Pseudonames are the Best" (Eye 1258). Is it not just typical of the Bosch to claim superiority in Pseudo Names?

ALAIN ZONFONT
DELLA PAT RHEA.

...Jane and I were offended by the entry this week (Eye 1258) which made fun of the German National Anthem. This was in very poor taste and we hope you will not accept similar contributions in the future.

TARZAN STRIPES.

...Though I love it to bits and look forward to its appearance in every issue, I'm not at all sure what the highly cultured Chinese would make of your Pseudo Names section.

RHODA BORROCKS.

...It has been a very cold winter here. I should have stayed at home.

S. KEYMOE-NELLE.

...As I deplore sloppy speech and lazy turns of phrase, I have found my own name an embarrassment. This has become worse since marrying into Ugandan society.

JUNO WATT
(now) JUNO WATT-AMIN.

...I feel my compatriots Frau Schland and Herr Berralles (Pseudo Names, Eye 1258) are letting the side down. As proud EU members, we should remember that we are all in this together.

YUL NEFFER-VOLK (Cologne).

...Your Pseudo Names section makes us want to jig with delight when we read it.

AMIN DAHMOUD
FURDAN SINGH.

...Here in China we look forward to the outcome of your latest experiment in democracy.

HUNG PA,
LI MEN.

...As a person of Irish-German descent, I wonder how long you hope to keep the international version of this feature airborne.

RYAN (HERR).

...I thank Rhoda Borrocks for her concern (Pseudo Names, Eye 1259), but Chinese people are not easily offended.

CHIN UP.

...Over here in Holland your stupid English preoccupation with daft Pseudo Names is driving us crazy. It's enough to make us swear!

RUUD VAN DRIVA.

...In Germany, we see Pseudo Names as just a passing fancy.

HERR TODAY,
GUNTER MORROW.

...I think that in the interest of European harmony, we simply cannot allow our German friends to dominate Pseudo Names. I really do think that it would be appreciated if the French were allowed some space as well.

MERCY BO KOO.

...Germans!!! Don't mention the war.

DEL B, LOU BIRDS, O FERR
D WHITE, CLIFF STOFDOVER.

...Readers from the international community are in high spirits over those Pseudo Names.

(SHEIKH) ATTAIL FETHA.

...On behalf of all expatriate-Aussie readers of Private Eye, I would like to thank you for your most amusing and educational Pseudo Names contributions.

GORDON U. MAITS.

...Why oh why are we bailing out the Greeks? My formidable mother would never have let them get away with it!

MA 'STRICT' TWEETY.

...Your "Pseudo Names International" section is deeply offensive to foreign persons. Keep up the good work.

RACHEL DISCRIMINATION.

...As a proud Yorkshireman of Chinese/Irish parents, I applaud your continued support of this multi-national column. The only problem I have is that I'm often frowned at when I identify myself by name.

FOO KINNELL.

...Mercy Bo Koo has got it wrong about Pseudo Names International (Eye 1262). They simply highlight our depressing inability to pronounce foreign names correctly. I doubt if this will stop it plodding on for decades, like those terrible West End musicals.

LES MISERABLES.

...Ah, votre organ magnifique. J'adore reading it quand je suis sur la plage.

PHILIPPE FALOPPE.

...News of the fall of the UK government has got many of us here in the Middle East putting on our dancing shoes.

YASSIR I. KHAN-BUGHI.

...As a young poet of mixed Indian/British descent I'd appreciate your support for my candidacy for the post of Oxford Professor of Poetry, especially as my cousin on my father's side is, I believe, a regular contributor to your magazine.

VIJAY THRIBB, 17.

...I wonder if there will be any Pseudo Names in the forthcoming FIFA World Cup? I certainly got a mention in the press for my goal-scoring prowess in the 1966 North Korean team and hope the current team are as equally heralded.

BANG WON IN.

...We were wondering if any of your international correspondents have the same trouble trying to communicate with their youth that the British and Americans do?

ANN I. WOZLYKE, OMAR GODD.

...I am fed up with the reputation my countrymen have for middle of the road music and a bland lifestyle. Right from the start I feel my destiny has been to live life right on the edge.

BJÖRN TOBI WILD.

...We Germans are sorry that we ended your World Cup dream and put paid to your ability to celebrate further into the summer...

KAI BOSCH.

...World Cup fever has arrived in Lhasa. Although televisions are banned in our mountain-top Tibetan temple, I talk through the matches with our monks each evening, and offer them the wisdom of my opinions on tactics and players.

PUNH DHITT.

...I was inspired to hear of Bang Won In's previous association with a successful World Cup side. I was hopeful of being contacted myself by one of the perhaps less prolific teams in the current competition, but sadly haven't heard anything yet.

AVA SHOTT (MRS).

...Watching England's soccer team commit professional football suicide was gut wrenching.

HARRY KIRRY.

...Je ne pense pas que toutes ces International Pseudo Names sont vrais. Peut être they should be checked par des experts avant publication.

PIERRE REVUE.

RAOUL MOAT

Was the Eye's Coverage Over The Top?

QUESTIONS have been asked over whether we gave over too much space to reporting on the manhunt which led up to the demise of the gunman Raoul Moat.

Our deployment of 500 journalists and camera teams to provide rolling 24-hour live coverage of Mr. Moat's death has in some quarters been questioned as possibly excessive.

Our 94-page supplement "Psycho on the Run" with full colour close-ups of his dead body, along with 40 pages of exclusive interviews with local people as they "try to come to terms with the unprecedented tragedy which has engulfed their close-knit Northumbrian community", was seen as a

tasteless intrusion into his private grief.

We reject these unwarranted misrepresentations of our coverage of this very important, significant and indeed iconic episode in British history, which tells us almost everything we need to know about the state of modern Britain.

We explain this in our 994-page fully illustrated souvenir pull-out booklet "Moat: The People's Nutter", with free DVD showing the last three hours of Moat's life, including tasers, suicide etc.

TOMORROW: **Eye Special Offer "RAOUL MOAT MOAT"** – a DIY defensive water feature to place around your home. Only £399 (*Water not included*).

POLICE LOG

Neasden Central Police Station

8.32 hrs All officers not still looking for suspect Raoul Moat to report for compulsory Dress Retraining Seminar in main locker room. Inspector Knicker of Scotland Yard will personally supervise Higher Level Personal Tidiness Management Exercises including the following:

1. Tying shoelaces (double knot).
2. Tucking shirt into trousers (if waistline permits).
3. Removal of non-issue items from utility belt (KFC bucket, packet 20 Benson & Hedges, copy of Loaded magazine, lead piping, 45 Magnum – slightly melted).
4. Wearing regulation helmet (ie. not balaclava, I ♥ Neasden baseball cap, Ku Klux Klan hood, etc.)

Course will last 2 hours followed by stress counselling for those officers traumatised by the introduction of the New Tidiness regime. Counselling session to be held in the Star of Helmand Halal Curry Emporium.

1200 hrs Annual leave begins.

Last Jonathan Ross TV Show ever until all the other ones he is going to do very soon

YES television will never be the same again until it is. Jonathan Ross has finally given up being a chat show host and will concentrate on his new career of being a chat show host.

It's the end of a new beginning. The old formula of making smutty jokes and sucking up to celebrities

is over. Instead viewers can expect to see a new formula of sucking up to celebrities while making smutty jokes.

"It's all change," said ITV's boss Peter Pinchem. "The days of Wossie being overpaid on BBC are over. Now he will be overpaid on ITV."

Tonight's TV Film

The Third Mandy adapted from the best-selling Memoirs of Lord Mandelson "The Third Man". Harry Slime (Peter Mandelson) is the man they thought was dead but he keeps coming up through the sewers to surprise his old friends. The police are on his tail but Slime lives in the shadows and is always a step ahead. Watch out for the iconic scene where Slime goes up in the London Eye and then jumps into the House of Lords. And don't miss the most famous movie line of all "500 years of democracy and they end up with me. They must be cuckoo".

Cast In Full

Harry Slime	Peter Mandelson
Gordon Brown	Joseph Cotton
Tony Blair	Trevor Howard
Man on Zither	David Frost

All together now '*Dunk-a-Dunk-a-Dunk A-Dunk...*'

"Whoa! Too much information"

"Come on – stop mucking about!"

From The Message Boards

Members of the online community respond to the major issues of the day...

Richard Dawkins condemns the burka

The sign at my brother's pub in Loughton says "No work clothes, no armed forces in uniform, no football colours, no Stone Island, no Burberry, no Boden, no burkas". And before you call him racist he's married to a coloured lady and she agrees with it. She's no oil painting but he wouldn't dream of making her hide her face in public – he'd rather we all suffered! Only kidding Pam, you look great (in the dark!)
– *Cyril_the_cabbie*

theres some well fit muslim bird's but theres some minger's out there whu need to wear a burka 😊 and a paper bag underneath in case it falls off! lol! – *Danny_Daz*

A muslim woman sat next to me on the tube today in order to surreptitiously read my newspaper. It's difficult to prove, because her veil shaded her eyes, but I distinctly heard her "tut" when I turned the page before she had finished an article on Afghanistan. I told her to buy her own copy, because if everyone read the Guardian without paying it would go out of business and there would be no national newspaper to represent enlightened opinion. – *Emily*

Maybe have burka's for children so paedo's cant look at them?
– *Save_Our_Kids*

but small peados wud disgise thereselves in burkas and mingle with the kids – *Think_about_it*

Any short arse in a burka comes near my kids I swear Ill do time
– *Family_Man*

Let's all boycott muslim eggs.
– *Winnie*

And muslim bacon! – *Danny_Daz*

And muslim Murray Mints!
– *Murray_Maniac*

Great stuff guys! – *Bogbrush*

TALES OF THE NOT VERY UNEXPECTED

Let me sell you a Tory

EXCLUSIVE TO PRIVATE EYE

The most sensational political memoirs ever written in the history of the world

In *The Third Mandy*, Peter Mandelson rips away the veil of secrecy that for 13 years shrouded the New Labour Government and for the first time reveals that:

○ **Tony Blair didn't like Gordon Brown**

○ **Gordon Brown didn't like Tony Blair**

○ **Gordon wanted Tony's job**

○ **Tony wouldn't give it to him**

What they said about each other

○ **Tony on Gordon:**
"I didn't like Gordon"

○ **Gordon on Tony:**
"I didn't like Tony"

The man who was there and saw it with his own eyes now tells it in his own words. Now read on:

CHAPTER 1
How I Was Right And Everyone Else Was Wrong

I'm going to let you into a little secret. Once upon a time there were three men who were in charge of everything.

And only one of them, Peter, was any good or had any idea what to do.

The other two, Tony and Gordon, spent all their time squabbling.

And Peter, had to spend all his time trying to clear up the messes they were making of everything.

Hence his private nickname 'The Turd Man'.

If only he had been the one they had picked to be prime minister in the first place.

How much better it would all have turned out.

But it's not too late, you know, for this fairy tale to have a crappy ending after all. *(Surely "happy" ending? Ed.)*

GIRLS BLOUSE DEPT.

"Have you got this in 'big'"?

BIGGEST NHS REFORMS SINCE LAST TUESDAY

THE NHS was reeling today after the most wide ranging reforms to hit the service since last Tuesday hit the NHS.

"Sigh," said one doctor.

After the sigh, the Department of Health reacted instantly, and confirmed that the latest sweeping reforms should not affect anybody, as they would be swept away by new sweeping reforms due to be announced next Tuesday.

New Drink Guidelines For GPs

UNDER new guidelines issued today by the government, doctors will be obliged to inform patients how much alcohol they drink. Patients will be entitled to know exactly how many units their GP has consumed before examining them.

If the doctor admits to a figure of over 40 units before lunch, the patient will be encouraged to report the doctor to the General Medical Council, who may be drunk as well.

Said one doctor yesterday, "Thish ish an outrageoush slurr in my speech". *(Surely "on my reputation"? Ed.)*

HOW THE BRITISH CONSTITUTION WAS MADE

No. 94
The Pocket Borough

INCREDIBLE as it may seem today, in those days a very rich man could literally buy his way into Parliament by way of what was known as a "pocket borough".

One particularly notorious example concerned the constituency of Richmond in Surrey, which was acquired in this manner for the sum of £264,000 by a well-known gambler of the time, Sir Zachariah Goldsmith.

Sir Zachariah had inherited a fabulous fortune from his father, the billionaire fishpaste manufacturer, Sir Jammy Goldfish. He used his fortune to buy political influence on an enormous scale, which led to widespread protests from the "toff-bashing" radicals of the day.

The leader of the Conservative Party Sir David Cameron, a close friend of Sir Zachariah's from their school days at Eton, was so swayed by the force of their protests that he did nothing at all.

■ For full Revision Notes on History GCSE: Part 94, go to our website: easypass.co.uk/nationalcurriculum

IRANIAN STONING WOMAN 'CONFESSES'

by Our Man In Tehran **Michael Burqa**

AN Iranian woman condemned to death by stoning, has appeared on Iranian TV to plead guilty to crimes of being a woman.

"I cannot lie any longer, I am guilty of adult womanery," she shamefully admitted during an appearance on the top-rated Iranian reality programme show "Strictly Come Stoning".

Penalties for being convicted of being a woman in Iran include "being stoned to death", "being stoned almost to death then thrown on a burning pyre" and the more lenient option of "not being stoned to death because you've already been beaten to death".

Meanwhile, the Iranian Vice President, Mohammad Reza Rahimi, described the British as "inhuman idiots" and *(cont. p. 94)*

"Ha, ha! Look at his stupid glasses!"

HEATH

Let's Parlez Franglais!

Numéro 94
Sur Le Film Set De Woody Allen

Woody Pargs *(pour c'est lui)*: Take trente et un! Action!

Carla Bruni: Mais je n'ai pas any words dans cette scène!

Woody Pargs: Coupez! Vous avez ruined le take!

Carla Bruni: Mais qu'est-ce que j'ai fait this time, Monsieur Woogy?

Woody Pargs: All vouz avez to do, Carla, c'est to walk dans le shop puis walk out again avec la baguette! Ok? Understandez-vous? Take trente deux. Action!

Carla Bruni: Mais qu'est-ce que c'est mon motivation?

Woogy Pargs: Coupez! Sacre bleu! Carla, ma cherie, votre motivation est très simple – vous voulez work avec le famous directeur Woogy Pargs. Now gettez on avec it avant je vous donne the sac! Take trente trois! Action!

Carla Bruni: Mais qu'est-ce que c'est le motivation de la baguette?

Woogy Pargs: Coupez! Merde! Vous êtes useless!

Président Sarkozy *(pour c'est lui)*: How dare vous dites que Carla est useless! Elle

est le plus brilliant actress dans le monde!

Woogy Pargs *(à Carla)*: Qui est le creepy vieux homme qui aime hanging around les belles femmes qui sont far trop young pour lui?

Président Sarkozy *(à Pargs)*: C'est *vous*, Woogy! Vraiement vous êtes un pervert!

Woogy Pargs: Ah bon! Then vous me donnerez un medal comme Roman Polanski!

Sarkozy: Idiot!

Allen: Bâtard!

Sarkozy: Cochon!

Carla Bruni: Coupez!

© Le late Kilometres Kington.

UPFRONTERS
On the Beach!!

Private Eye's Definitive Guide to the Celebs on Holiday!!

■ Ooh! You are a **One Show Christine**! Let's be **Frank**, the future doesn't look too **Bleakley** for Mr **Lampard** at the moment as the couple frolic together in the South of France!

■ It's simple **Simon**! You just **Holden** to the lovely **Amanda** and you can be sure she won't give you the **Cowell-d** shoulder! Phew! It's the X-Factor here in the Caribbean!

■ Lovely **Cheryl** isn't giving you the **Cole** shoulder is she? *(You've done this one, Ed.)* Lucky for movie heartthrob **Di Caprio** that he has someone to **Leon-ordo** on for support!! "Hold me Titanic!" as they say here in France's Caribbean!

■ I'm all right **Jack**! Hell-raiser Nicholson certainly is, as he gives the French First Lady a helping hand with some sun cream. **Carla**'s going to be a lovely shade of **Bruni**! *(Are you sure about this, Ed?)* or maybe it's **Peter Stringfellow** and TV's **Davina McCall** – Yes, these two could create some Big Bother down in the South of the Caribbean!

■ For **Peter**'s sake put hunky singer **André** down, **Teri** – you look like a Desperate Housewife!! Is the American star **Hatcher**-ing a plan to grab **Jordan**'s ex for herself? *(Is this right? Ed.)* Perhaps not and the happy couple are in fact TV's **Gary Lineker** and newly single **Patsy Kensit** – Yes, it's Match of the Day here in the South Caribbean island of France! *(You're fired. Ed.)*

■ There's nothing like a **Dame**! And Ms **Mirren** is one **Helen** of a sight as she shows off her bikini figure in the South of French Caribbean! *(That's it. This time, you really are fired. Ed.)*

Why is the Clintons' daughter called Chelsea?

(Ian Fenbridge, Salop)

● There is a long tradition in America of naming children after favourite areas of London. When I was at school in the 1950s in New Dworkin fellow pupils (with whom I am still in contact) included Battersea Plimsoll and Fulham G. Heidelberg. One of our next door neighbours in Philadelphia was (Ms.) Camberwell Goldsmith who was married, by an extraordinary coincidence, to Notting-Hill-Gate Munchausen.

Prof. X.J. Meinsweeper.

● Is Professor Meinsweeper trying to hoax you readers with his laughable stories of Americans christened Notting-Hill-Gate and Battersea? Chelsea has nothing to do with the London borough of that name but derives from the Sussex village of Winchelsea from which many early immigrants to America hailed. In their new home many adopted the name of their place of origin – the 'Win' being later dropped.

F.C. Whittam-Smith.

● I hesitate to contradict Mr(?) Whittam-Smith but I refer him and others to Kitty Kelley's authoritative life of Hillary Clinton, *Hillary*. On p.4,617 you may read how the former President, a fan of Chelsea Football Club from his student days in the UK and considerably the worse for wear at his daughter's christening, insisted that his child should bear the name of Chelsea.

R.P. McStrange.

Answers please to the following:

What is Eric Pickles real name? Can you get a B* at A Level? Does anyone read the Economist?

DIARY

JOAN COLLINS

Sun, sea and sand. St Tropez in August – or Aout, as we know it over here – must surely be the most glamorous place on earth.

I first came here with Rudolph Valentino, and, a little later, with the equally naughty Lionel Barrymore. In those days, anyone who was anyone made a bee-line for La Trop – King Teddy VII and Sarah Bernhardt to name but two.

And today, once more, le tout monde est ici! Only yesterday, I visited one of my very favourite eateries on the French Riviera, the splendid Chez Nous, in the A-list company of top director Michael Winner, top novelist Lord Jeffrey Archer and top composer Lord Andrew Lloyd-Webber.

I arrived a little late. "You look twenty-five years young, Joanie!" the men chorused as I made my entrance, causing all heads to turn, "How on earth do you do it?"

RADA-trained, I left a theatrical thirty seconds before removing my luxury fur stole to reveal a plunging diamond-studded neckline on my glamorous mauve ballgown with its extravagant shoulder pads (yes, they're "in" again, or so I'm assured by my friends in the shoulder pad industry!). Then, looking over my shoulder, fluttering my eyelashes, showing some thigh and winking, I purred "You want to know the secret, gents? One word – CLASS!".

Sadly, these days it's not a word you hear much of.

And whatever happened to good manners? The last time I entered an old favourite Mayfair restaurant, I headed straight for the best table, as one was always taught to do – but the overweight slobs who were occupying it (complete unknowns) resolutely refused to get up and move!

I got my own back by staging a spillage of tomato soup over their cheap suits and hideous Viyella dresses. But is their loutish display the best we can do for chivalry in the 21st century? Quel horror! as the infinitely more stylish French would say.

What's to be done about the looming double-dip recession? Simple. Pass laws to forbid the wearing of those dreadfully ugly "trainers", and thus force the riff-raff to shell out oodles more cash on decent shoes, such as proper glamorous high-heels full of sex appeal. Result? A massive upturn for Britain's vital shoe industry, and a shot in the arm for the worldwide economy. But today's politicians, so out of touch with reality, seem incapable of coming up with such an obvious solution.

May one ask a rude question? Whatever happened to glamour?

In my day, the world was full of the most glamorous people. Diana Dors, Dickie Henderson, Noele Gordon, Little Arthur Askey (NOT so little where it matters, incidentally!) and my own good self, to name but a few. There was nothing coarse, smutty or unseemly about us. Far from it. We exuded glamour. More importantly, we knew how to conduct ourselves in public.

The truth is that most of today's TV is coarse, repellent, amateurish and puerile. And, as I made clear on Channel 5's excellent Topless from Studio 5 the other day, the reason is that it's all driven by tacky reality shows that feed off these people who are so thilled to be on TV they'll appear for the price of a train ticket – if they even get that much for their trouble. They all think they have what it takes to be a star – as if they knew the true meaning of the word!

Does anyone really care about these half-baked celebrities who whip off their clothes at the drop of a hat and indulge in ludicrous "sex games" while pretending not to be aware of the camera?

In my day, filming some of the great movies from the heyday of cinema – and I'm talking now of classic movies like The Stud – one would never have dreamed of wearing what I believe are known as "jeans" or a "tank-top". No, we had more respect for ourselves that that. But the young these days think that simply by wearing tacky clothes and then "stripping off for the camera" they are entitled to call themselves stars.

What baloney! It certainly wasn't like that in my day!

To my eye, today's so-called "beautiful people" – raddled Kate Moss, pudgy Angelina Jolie and the ubiquitous two-a -penny Kylie, to name but a few – look more like raddled old bag-ladies than true stars.

Whatever happened to good old-fashioned sex appeal?

Whenever I dine at the five star restaurants like The Wolesley I quiz my fashionable male dinner-companions such as top journalist Andrew Neil, top actor Roger Moore, top Captain of Industry Lord Sugar and top TV moghul Richard Desmond as to who they find the more appealing, myself or the three above-mentioned slags. "No contest!" they all say, as I beckon for the bill.

What's to be done about the infamous oil-slick off the Florida coastline? It's brown, it's rich, it's oily and it's everywhere.

C'mon, girls – never heard of tanner? Joan's Top Tip: scoop up some slick, sloosh it on all over, and – hey presto! – you'll look as truly sensational as the glamorous and miraculously still-young Hollywood stars of yesteryear.

As told to CRAIG BROWN

First Unborn Baby Ever To Get A* GCSE In Nuclear Physics

**By Our Education Staff
Lunchtime O'Levels**

UNBORN toddler Vikram Dunwoody, aged 0, has this year become the youngest ever candidate to be awarded top A* marks in a GCSE science paper.

Says his mother Mrs Vedanta Dunwoody, "We always knew that little Vikram was going to be a high-flyer when he was born but in doing so well even before he had come into the world, he has surpassed even our expectations."

Everyone a Michael Winner

"We very much hope that by the time he is seven he will have enough qualifications to become one of Mr William Hague's ever-growing band of special advisers."

Young Vikram's success coincides with record results for several million other candidates in this year's GCSE exams.

More than 110 percent of candidates scored A* or higher, and the number of failures for the first reached zero.

On Other Pages ● NO PICTURES OF SPOTTY BOYS EXPERIENCING ECSTASY AS THEY LEARN OF THEIR RECORD PASSES *p. 1* ● GOVE APOLOGISES FOR RESULTS MIX-UP *p. 16*

GCSEs WARNING

FRUITY GIRLS celebrating passing their GCSEs have been warned of increased competition for places on the front page of the Daily Telegraph.

"Where once just wearing a pretty blouse and a sensible skirt was enough to guarantee you a decent place on page 1 that's sadly no longer the case," said one Daily Telegraph sub-editor. "This year you'll require at least one cut-off midriff top and a light cottony

skirt to ensure a place."

"Unless your outfit gets at least a "Phwoar, she's a cracker" from the sub's desk, you don't stand a chance of getting anywhere near the front page".

"You can leave your CV if you want, but most jobs have been outsourced"

Duchess of Love...

by Dame Sylvie Krin

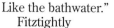

THE STORY SO FAR: Charles has launched a new initiative to promote "Practical Sustainable Living". Now read on...

Camilla was luxuriating in her morning bath surrounded by a veritable phalanx of bottles of exotic bath–time unguents, *Dr.Stuttaford's Canadian Pine Needle Rheumatic Balm, Mitchell and Webb's Menthol Muscle Relaxant, Hayward's Louisiana Pelican Oil...* And above the mélange of all these delicious odours wafted the unmistakable tang of her full strength Trident Untipped Navy shag.

"Mmmm" She sighed contentedly (as she listened with half an ear to the spiritual homily of Rabbi Blue on her Digital Andrew Roberts Radio as he reminisced in his soothing tones about the meatballs his old Lithuanian grandmother once made for him.

However her reverie was disturbed by an agitated knocking on the door accompanied by the familiar voice of her royal husband.

"Are you still there old thing? Whatever you do, don't pull the plug out!!"

"What on earth are you talking about Chazza?" Camilla rasped, annoyed that her hour of tranquillity had been so rudely interrupted.

"Er... It's part of my new plan for everyone to sort of do their bit to save the planet"

She groaned inwardly. What would it be this time?

"We are going to recycle the bathwater and pour it on the garden," said Charles excitedly.

"What? With me in it?" she retorted, as the long column of ash fell off her cigarette into the foam with a faint sizzle.

"No. No. You silly old goose. You get out and Fitztightly will organise the whole thing with his bucket. You see, I've taken a leaf out of Prince Albert's book, he was my great–great–great–great thingy and er..."

Charles and Camilla were dining alone in the Mountbatten Banqueting Suite. The strong evening sunlight pierced remorselessly through the leaded windows.

"What have you done with the curtains Chazza?" Camilla asked, blinking in the unaccustomed glare.

"I've had them taken down and turned into fashionable handbags, you know, to carry thingies around in!"

"It's another one of my recycling ideas. Like the bathwater."

Fitztightly coughed politely and enquired, "Will you both be having the vegetarian option this evening, sire? Fresh vegetables from the garden, we picked them only this morning".

"Oh rather! They always taste so much better when they come out of the earth," Charles enthused as his faithful equerry piled a cornucopia of parsnips, carrots, radishes and beetroot onto his plate.

"Hang on," Charles cried suddenly, "this dressing smells pretty odd!"

"I haven't put any dressing on, Sire." Fitztightly protested. "In accordance with your instructions about the need to cut down on imports of foreign olive oil."

"But this carrot tastes all soapy! And the beetroot smells of Menthol! And the parsnips reek of pine needles? And what's this?"

Charles held up his fork and there on the end was the unmistakable sodden butt of a full strength Trident Untipped Navy Shag cigarette.

Suddenly the golden sunlight disappeared behind a cloud and the first drops of rain spattered against the curtainless window...

(To be continued)

The Alternative Rocky Horror Service Book

No. 94 Service For A Marriage Of Convenience between Two Persons Who Have Not Previously Met.

Reverend Brown *(for it is he)*: Brothers and sisters, we are gathered here in the sight of God, and no-one else because it is a Wednesday morning, to join together in Holy Matrimony N and M *(it may be Onanugu and Margazja or similar)*. Marriage is an Holy estate ordained by God for the purposes of bringing men and women together in the country of their choice so that they may enjoy the full benefits of living in Britain *(N and M shall then give a sign that they understand what is being said)*.

Reverend Brown: Who giveth away this woman to this man? *(at this point the Agent shall step forward, it may be Dmitri Mafioski or some such similar responsible personage)*.

The Agent: I do.

Reverend Brown: Who giveth me the brown envelope with a contribution to aid the Roof Fund?

The Agent: I do. As agreed *(here the Agent may make a suitable offering, it may be £1,000, £2,000 or similar sum)*.

Offertory Hymn

The congregation (3) shall sing "I vow to thee my new country"

Reverend Brown: If anyone knows of any just cause or impediment why these two strangers should not be joined together in Holy Matrimony you are advised to keep quiet because our friend here *(he may then indicate the Agent again)* knoweth where you livest.

The Marriage

Reverend Brown: Do you N take this woman M to be your lawful wedded wife, to have and to hold until this service is over?

N: Ok, yes, Sir.

Reverend Brown: And do you M take this man as your lawful wedded husband so long as you both shall be in the church?

M: Da, innit?

Reverend Brown: You may now kiss the Bride goodbye.

There shall then follow a suitable piece of music possibly Wagner's Bribal March.

HOLMES GAGS BBC SKETCH SHOW

I'm really thin-skinned

Stop throwing your weight about

Fat lot of good that will do

Captions by Lunchtime O'Bese and Phil Belly

Nursery Times

Friday, August 6, 2010

COCK ROBIN KILLING

CPS claim insufficient evidence to prosecute sparrow

by Our Rhyme Staff
Polly Put The Kettle On

THE Crown Prosecution Service last night announced that it would not be taking action against PC Sparrow over the death of Cock Robin.

Mr Robin was hit by an arrow and died shortly afterwards, but his assailant PC Sparrow was seen by an eye witness.

Said Mr Fly, "I saw him die and I captured it on my little eye-phone."

Mr Fly handed over footage to the Nursery Times of PC Sparrow deliberately aiming his bow and arrow at Cock Robin, but last night the CPS said that Mr Fly's film was "insufficient evidence with which to proceed".

A spokesman said, "There is no conclusive proof whether Cock Robin died from the arrow through the heart or whether he was generally feeling a bit poorly."

Friends of Cock Robin were outraged at this miscarriage of justice. Said one, "All the birds of the air were a-sighing and a-sobbin' when they heard of the murder of poor Ian Tomlinson."

Those Key Qualities BP Was Looking For In Tony Hayward's Successor

■ Bob Dudley is American.

■ He's an American, born in America.

■ With an American passport.

■ Did we mention that he's an American?

■ American born and bred. Yessiree. Born in the good old U.S. of A.

■ As American as apple pie or deep water drilling off the Gulf of Mexico.

■ Er... That's it.

Hayward's End

"Looks like we've got another gusher!"

On Your Bike!!!

A message from London's Mayor

What ho, Londoners. Boris has come up with an absolutely first-rate boffo scheme! Well, I borrowed it from Johnny Frog, if the truth be told – which it isn't very often in my case, ha ha ha!

Anyway let me explain how Bojo's "On yer bike" scheme works.

Say you wanted to get from your office to the flat of a lady friend round the back of Totty Court Road. You hire a bike from one of my new "bike docks", jump on it, cycle round to lady friend and then jump on her.

Then you do it again! It's simple! You get your leg over your bike and then you get your leg over the totty.

And the brilliant thing is that you can do it all over London.

Eventually, you can back-pedal all the way home and tell the missus you've been working late on your bicycle scheme!

Put it this way, chums, it keeps you fit. It's good for the planet. And it doesn't cost anything – not even my job!

So that's my message to all you Londoners. Get bonking with Boris! *(Surely "biking"? Ed.)* And thanks to our sponsors, Barclays Bonk *(Surely "bike"? Ed.)*.

Issued by the Office of the London Mayor 2010

The Amazing Things We Now Know About The Afghan War Thanks To The Internet Leak Of Thousands Of Highly Classified Documents

☐ The effectiveness of the Taliban's guerilla campaign was woefully misjudged by American commanders

☐ Terrible flaws in the coalition strategy are resulting in the unnecessary deaths of hundreds of allied troops

☐ Pakistan only pays lip service to supporting the American mission so as to enjoy billions of dollars in aid

☐ Thousands of Afghan civilians have been killed by coalition blunders

☐ The war is unwinnable

☐ The Pope really is a Catholic

☐ Bears do actually shit... *(That's enough. Ed)*

WHITE HOUSE FURY AT AFGHANISTAN LEAKS

I blame BP

Workers Allowed To Continue Working After Death

The Government's decision to abolish laws preventing people working on after their death has been widely welcomed by the huge population of the hard-working deceased.

"When I died I was thrown into a hole and covered with dirt," said 94-year-old Graham Cooper. "I felt like they were doing this to me for no other reason than I was dead. It was appalling."

Public Given Freedom To Do The Things Nobody Wants To Do

There was widespread joy throughout Britain today as the Government delivered on its promise to give people the freedom to do for themselves all the things that none of them want to do.

"Labour's nanny state is dead; we can now police our own streets, teach our children ourselves in schools we set up and run ourselves and, from next year, we'll even be able to perform our own operations on ourselves at home," said one delighted Bradford man (cont. p. 94)

Coalition Message To Those Claiming Disability Living Allowance

Get on your bike

Britain's 50 best car parks

43 Neasden Tesco

Good disabled access. Pay 'n' display. 37 bays. Free parking for Tesco customers. Remember to keep receipt.

44 NCP Droitwich

One of the Midlands' finest multi-storey carpark. Adjacent to station and Droitwich's award-winning Octagon shopping complex. Superb view of downtown Droitwich from Level 3.

45 Auchtermuchty

The smallest car park in Britain. The "Wee-wee Mac-Car Park" has space for only one small car. A must-see for the car park aficionados.

46 Croydon General Hospital

Huge former bomb site now Grade II listed. Europe's most expensive parking facility – but well worth the £13.70 an hour. Regular shuttle service takes you to hospital (subject to availability).

47 Beaulieu National Car Park Museum Car Park

Britain's oldest car park in the grounds of this famous stately home takes you on a trip to a bygone age of carparks where you are allowed to smoke and there are no CCTV cameras.

48 Mansfield Park Opera

Temporary car park in field adjoining famous stately home. Opera lovers speak highly of the complimentary tractor facility when cars get stuck in the famous mud of the former potato field.

49 Stansted Long Stay Car Park

This state-of-the-art complex, visible from outer space, can accomodate 1,000,000 cars. Sat-nav navigation is compulsory. Legend tells of "The Stansted Ghost", a short haul commuter to Preston who died after a two month search for his car. "Not to be missed" – TV's Simon Schama.

50 Lymeswold-on-Sea

Clifftop Wildlife Park. Breathtaking views of the crumbling coastline. But beware! Lymeswold County Council warns parkers that they take no responsibility for cars that plunge 130 feet into the so-called "Graveyard of the Cars" caused by coastal erosion. Hurry while car park lasts.

Is your favourite car park in our list? Let us know at Indieborefeatures. *Next week:* 50 Favourite Trouser Presses

---

THE WORD CLOUD> by Wordle >

The size of the words indicates the frequency of their use by readers of the **Independent**

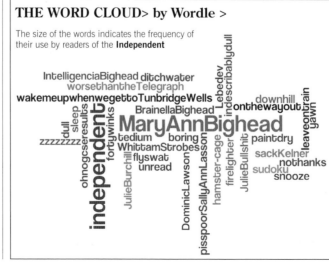

"Turn around when possible, Dick Whittington"

CONTROVERSIAL TOPSHOP BOSS JOINS GOVERNMENT

I'm a rough diamond

Sounds good to me!

I'll be looking closely at the figures

Cheeky!

WORLD OF SOCCER
NEW INJUNCTION SHOCK

by **E.L. Erewego** Our Man Outside The Changing Room Denied Admittance

A **FURTHER** injunction was imposed last night at the request of a Neasden footballer – bringing the number of injunctions successfully applied for to eleven.

The player, who cannot be named for legal reasons, is believed to be involved in a personal capacity in behaviour which cannot be disclosed.

Gagging For It

Said the ashen-faced manager who also cannot be named for legal reasons, "Everyone is entitled to live in privacy. What the players get up to with prostitutes and other players' wives... WHOOPS!"

The manager continued, "Be careful what you print as what I have just said is covered by a super-injunction, the reporting of which is also covered by an injunction, and this injunction is in turn covered by an injunction forbidding any reference to any such matter as all-night orgies and love romps in seedy hotels."

The man who cannot be named is 59.

Late Score

Neadsen 1
Another team that cannot be named...........17

Man of the match: Redacted

CAMPBELL 'LIED' AT WAR CRIMES TRIAL – WORLD IN SHOCK

by Our International Court Staff **Sara Leone**

WORLD famous celebrity Alastair Campbell today made headlines all over the world when he testified at the trial for the war crimes of Tony Blair, the deposed former dictator of the tiny and impoverished West European state, Great Britain.

Standing seemingly unrepentant in the witness box, Campbell described how he had been woken in the night by a mysterious figure who had handed him a dossier containing what he called "a number of dirty lies".

Campbell denied that he had later polished them up and sold them to the British public as an accurate record of Iraq's stockpile of weapons of mass destruction.

Blood Diamonds Are Forever

Sitting in the dock, protected by 150 armed policemen costing the taxpayers £1 billion a year, the alleged war criminal Mr Blair himself betrayed no emotion as Campbell trotted out what his lawyer, Lord Falconer, described as, "a tissue of untruths from beginning to end".

Lord Falconer told the court, "My client does not wish to comment at this stage because he plans to give a full account in his forthcoming book of memoirs in which he will refute these terrible lies of Mr Campbell's by telling much more interesting lies of his own."

'BRING THIS EVIL WARLORD TO JUSTICE', SAYS TAYLOR

by Libby Rhia

FORMER Liberian dictator Charles Taylor last night urged a specially convened court in The Hague to find supermodel Naomi Campbell guilty of war crimes and crimes against humanity for the bloody civil war in Sierra Leone which cost hundreds of thousands of lives.

"Like all decent right-thinking people I have been appalled by the sickening evidence we've heard this week against the evil despot Ms Campbell. I'm just glad she's the one on trial and not me" said a clearly relieved (cont. p. 94)

That Nelson Mandela 1997 Dinner Party – Who was there?

N. Mandela

Princess Diana (the late)

Jemima Puddleduck and her then husband Mr Imran Fox

Mia Farrow and her then husband Mr Frank Sinatra (the late)

Mr Neil "Blood" Diamond

Supermodel Marilyn Monroe

Sir Stephen Fry

Adolf Hitler, the alleged war criminal (surely "Charles Taylor, the little-known Liberian mass-murderer? Ed.)

"I see the schools have gone back"

POLLY FILLER

SO Emma Thompson says that women "can't have it all"! Really, Emma! Are you telling me that I can't be a good mum *and* work full-time as the country's leading columnist on the problems of being a good mum and working full-time?

Well, purleeease!

Here in the Filler household we certainly don't need any lectures from dyed-blonde-haired film stars (!!) about how to juggle our lives!!

And actually, Emma, it *is* possible for women to have it all and there are some very good examples right in front of you, if you would only stop going to Oscar ceremonies, dyeing your hair blonde and LOOK!!!

YES, dear, there *are* women who have satisfying careers, are in happy relationships with their useless partners (even though they sit around watching Extreme Dressage with Zara Phillips on Sky Sport 94 all day... forget it, Simon, you're not even *nearly* in her league) and who, of course,

are wonderful (naturally blonde!!) mothers to their bright, gifted, happy and well-rounded toddlers.

I don't want to boast, but when I picked up Charlie from his three-week Suzuki Violin Swimming and Woodcraft Boarding Summer Camp Experience, he proved what a funny, original and clever child he is, reducing everyone to tears of laughter by asking, "Are you the new au pair?".

Hilarious (even though I don't look anything like our useless new girl, Oxfama from Pakistan) and of course available in my new collection of amusing anecdotes from the front line of modern motherhood, *Shut Up Emma And Get Yourself A Nanny – For A Small McPhee!!* (£19.99, Candy, Pearson & Johnson).

THE NEW NORTH-SOUTH DIVIDE
Is the gap widening?

'I NEVER SLEPT WITH LYNN BARBER' claims Oxford Man

by Our University Staff
Don Giovanni

THE WORLD of Academe was stunned last night by the shock claim of a former Oxford undergraduate who told reporters that he had never been to bed with the young Lynn Barber.

The man who did not want to be named (Septimus Tweedy, Classics at Keeble 1959-1962) said "I know it was the thing to do at Oxford and everyone else was sleeping with Lynn Barber all the time but I wanted to rebel against all that and go punting, attend choral evensong and take ladies out for tea."

Stupid Punt

However his claims have been met with some scepticism by his peers. Said one "If what Tweedy says is true then he would have to have gone a total of 9 terms, that is 72 entire weeks at Oxford without having sex with Lynn Barber. That's just not possible.

DIG FOR LIBTORY!!
Fountain and Jamieson

Nursery Times

Friday, September 3, 2010

'WE'RE NOT FIGHTING EACH OTHER', say Tweedle brothers

by Our Political Correspondents **Millie** and **Molly Band**

THE two contestants for the Labour throne, Dave Tweedledum and Ed Tweedledee have vowed not to attack each other.

But today the gloves were off as Mr Bean lookalike Dave Tweedledum hit out at his brother with a rattle.

But younger brother Tweedledee demanded "fair play" and promised not to hit below the belt.

"Unlike my brother, I will make it a clean contest", he said. "I will not mention the fact that Dum is rather weird and does funny things with bananas."

That Honorary Degree Citation In Full

SALUTAMUS REBEKAM WADEM CELEBRATA RUFA EDITRIX QUOTIDIANENSIS JOURNALIS "SOL" (APPELATUS "CURRENTUS BUNNUS" POPULARI) PROPRIETORO ANTIPODENSIS RUPERTO MURDOCHO ALIAS "SQUALIDUS DIGGERUS" REBEKA FLAGELLATOR PAEDOPHILORUM EST QUOS DICARIT FAMOSISSIMA "STRINGENDI SUNT – EST SOLA LINGUA QUOD COMPREHENDUNT" QUONDAM INCARCERATA ERAT PRO DOMESTICA VIOLENCIA CONTRA UXOREM ROSSUM KEMPUM ACTORIS IN OPERA SAVONA PISSPOORA "EASTENDERENSIS" SED NUNC MARITUS AD CAROLUS BROOKUS TUTOR EQUORUM ET TIPSTERUS DODGIUS MAXIMUS, ET ELEVATA QUA DOMINATRIX SUPREMISSIMA IN CORPORATIONIS "NOVIS INTERNATIONALIBUS" ET DEXTERO FEMINA AD SQUALIDUM DIGGERUM GAUDEAMUS DIGGERTUR (GEDDITUR?)!

© UNIVERSITY OF THE ARTS LONDON (FORMERLY THE GROUCHO CLUB) 2010.

A Taxi Driver writes

EVERY week a well-known taxi driver is asked to comment on an issue of topical importance. This week Nobel Prizewinning cabbie **Sir Vidia Naipaul OM** (Cab No. 8910) on the sad condition of the African continent.

Ever been to Africa, guv? Take my advice, don't touch it with a barge pole! Those darkies haven't got a clue about anything. I dunno how they ever found their way down the trees in the first place. I went there once myself. I couldn't wait to get back to civilisation. Horrible smelly place, full of dead cats, dead lizards and stinking garbage. Do you know what I'd do to all those Africans? Send them back to where they came from. It would be the only language they could understand if they even had a language in the first place. I had that Nelson Mandela in the back of the cab once. Very cultured gentleman.

NEXT WEEK: JULIE BURCHILL (Cab No. 1234) on "Why the anti-obesity health fascists should all be strung up".

TV Highlights

BBC1, Sunday, 9.00pm

Sherlock

Holmes and Watson face their most baffling modern day mystery to date, when they are drafted in to decipher exactly how Mr. David Kelly really died.

"No fingerprints on the knife, Watson, and no gloves found on the body."

"But what does that mean Sherlock?"

"It means Lord Hutton has classified all the records for the next 70 years."

Eye rating – Hats off to the men from 221b (Norman) Baker Street!

ME AND MY SPOON

KATIE PRICE

Have spoons played a major part in your career?

I'm not answering that, 'cos it's all in my new book. You'll have to buy it.

Is that the latest volume of your autobiography "Me and My Pair of Enormous Spoons" by Katie Price?

Fuck knows! I haven't read it, have I?

Do you have a favourite spoon?

Yeah, but you'll have to watch my new reality show "What Katie Did Next With a Spoon". It's going to be on Channel 5 or maybe Channel 5 is the name of my new perfume... I can't remember... bollocks, anyway.

Has anything amusing ever happened to you in connection with a spoon?

Piss off. Why are you having a go at me? Oh yeah, let's everyone pick on Katie just 'cos she's worth £30 million... Tossers. I don't care, I've got a new range of baby spoons out called "Katie's Sexy Babe Spoons", so you can all *(Sadly, at this point, the interview had to be concluded, as Ms Price had to attend a pressing cage fight)*

NEXT WEEK: *A Good Read with Alex Reid.*

"Makes you feel sort of insignificant, doesn't it?"

ARE YOU MIDDLE CLASS?
Ten Tell-Tale Signs

1 You went to Eton.

2 You were a member of the Bullingdon Club at Oxford.

3 You are a direct descendent of William IV.

4 You are the 8th cousin of Boris Johnson.

5 You are married to the daughter of a Baronet and Viscountess.

6 You are the son of a wealthy stockbroker and a Justice of the Peace.

7 You are a millionaire several times over.

8 You made an expenses claim for "cutting back wisteria" at one of your agreeable homes.

9 You have tennis elbow (surely "sharp elbows"? Ed.)

10 You support Aston Villa (surely "fox hunting"? Ed.)

PAKISTAN SHAME

We've lost the match

All that remains is to play the game

HOW YOU CAN NOT GIVE TO REBUILD PAKISTAN

All over the world people haven't been moved by the images of flood ravaged Pakistan, and you can join them.

But what can you do not to help? Just like millions around the globe you can start by not donating any money. Not donating money couldn't be simpler. You can not donate money in the following ways:

● not giving money directly to the Disasters Emergency Committee.

● not setting up a direct debit to the Red Cross.

● hiding your face in the paper when someone rattles a tin near you.

It can be not giving as little as £1, or not giving as much £100*, what matters is that you help show this hotbed of terrorism that the West doesn't give two monkeys about it.

Remember, not giving money is completely tax-free.

Please remember not to tick the giftaid box when not giving your donation.

EXCITEMENT REACHES FEVER PITCH AS OLYMPICS LOOM

by Our Entire Staff **Lunchtime O'Lympics and Coe**

WITH the London Olympics only a mere two years away – that's 9,436,264 seconds and counting – the entire population of Britain is erupting in an unparalleled frenzy of eager anticipation.

Everyone, everywhere is united in a national fervour not seen since the heady days of the Hundred Years War.

Said a typical Stratford East-based newsagent, Sanjit Patel, 53, summing up the feelings of every Briton, "I cannot wait. It will be the greatest moment of my entire life – people coming from all over the world to visit my tiny shop to buy a can of Pepsi for £11.99. It is a dream come true."

Since you began reading this article, there are now only 9,436,150 seconds before the starting gun goes off to mark the opening of the Games with the start of the 20 kilometre underwater synchronised dressage event in Bournemouth.

The Olympic Games In Numbers

Cost of Olympic Velodrome **£2.4 million**

Hours of Olympic TV coverage **17.5 million**

Cost of protecting athletes from terrorist attack **£2.3 billion**

Cost of protecting Mr Boris Johnson from irate husbands, wives, girlfriends, etc **£4.6 billion**

Estimated number of visitors to Women's Weightlifting Arena **12.2 million**

Estimated number of visitors to Mr Patel's shop to buy Pepsi **7.6 billion**

Number of Wenlock Mascot souvenirs sold **3**

Number of articles recycling press release from Olympic Delivery Authority, saying how great the Games are going to be **216 million**

"Vince Cable is getting desperate"

That Security ~~Form~~ For The ~~Blair~~ Book Signing

CANCELLED

BLAIR IN CHARITY CASH SHOCK

I want to help rehabilitate injured ex-Prime Ministers *(surely "soldiers"? Ed)*

That Prescott Attack on Turncoat Milburn In Full

ALAN Milburn is nothing more than a collaborationist deliberately corroborating with a Tory government when he is supposited to be a membrane of the Labour Party where incrementally he can find a perfect demonscription of "social mobility" in the life of yours truly who started out as a humble Trade Unionist and ended up as a nobilised Lord in the Upper Chamberlain, so yah boo sucks to Milburn who clearly has no conscienscious, unlike some of us who supported the Irani war and shagged our *(cont. p. 94)*

COALITION ROCKED BY CLEGG GAFFE

by Our Political Staff **Quentin Lettscrackupcameron**

THE political world was rocked to its foundations yesterday when deputy prime minister Nick Clegg, standing in for David Cameron, dropped the biggest clanger in the history of Westminster.

MPs from all parties gasped when Clegg described the invasion of Iraq in 2003 as "illegal".

Said one seasoned political commentator (myself), "Clegg made the most elementary mistake that any politician can ever be guilty of – he told the truth."

Said another top Westminster analyst (also myself), "What a schoolboy howler. No wonder Lib Dem support is ebbing away to a mere 25 percent."

OBAMA CONFIRMS U.S. IRAQ PULLOUT

Mission unaccomplished